THE WISE
GALATIAN

WITH CONFESSIONS FROM A FOOLISH ONE

BEING COMPLETED IN THE HOLY SPIRIT

GEOFFREY GAY

Ark House Press
arkhousepress.com

© 2025 Geoffrey Gay

All rights reserved. Apart from any fair dealing for the purpose of study, research, criticism, or review, as permitted under the Copyright Act, no part may be reproduced by any process without written permission.

Unless otherwise stated, all scriptures are quoted from the
The Holy Bible: The New King James Version (NKJV) (1983)
Thomas Nelson Inc., Nashville TN.
or from the Concordant Literal New Testament (Con Lit NT) (1978)
Concordant Publishing Concern, Canyon County CA.

Cataloguing in Publication Data:
Title: The Wise Galatian: *with confessions from a foolish one*
ISBN: 978-1-7640298-3-4 (pbk)
Subjects: REL012120   RELIGION / Christian Living / Spiritual Growth; REL095000   RELIGION / Christian Education / Adult; REL006720   RELIGION / Biblical Studies / New Testament / Paul's Letters.

Design by initiateagency.com

CONTENTS

PART ONE ~ BACKGROUND 1
   Foolish Galatians Anonymous 3
   'Mission Drift' In Asia Minor 5
   The Original Drift 7
   'The Man On The Middle Cross' 10
   Driving Instructions 12

PART TWO ~ SHAKY GROUND 15
   Meanwhile, Back In Turkiye... 17
   Law 19
      • *Getting The Right Answer!* *19*
   Perry Mason In Sandals 21
   Defining Law 23
   Law As Compulsion 25
   Further Insights? 27
   Three Types Of Law 28
      • *Concerning Compulsion* *30*
   The Beginning Of Law 31
      • *Is God's Law Forever?* *33*
   Commands – The Ultimate Laws And Purposes? 35
   The Purpose Of The Law According To Paul In Galatians 38
      • *Concerning The Word 'Under'* *41*
   The Galatian Corollaries 42
      • *Punishment 'Under Law'* *45*
      • *Concerning Boundaries* *47*
   A Final Word On Law 51
   Legalism 53
   Desiring To Be Under Law 55
   Legalism As A Mentality Or Mindset 58
   Reverence Versus Religion / Ritual 60
   Legalism As Evangelism 62
   No Legalism In Relationship 64
      • *Concerning Children* *67*
   The Preachers Who Knew Enough! 69

Licence	71
• *Concerning Anarchy*	*73*
The Venn Diagram For Soul-Swingers	77
Legalism, Licence And Soul-Swinging!	79
• *Concerning The Study Of The 'Mind'*	*83*
Sample Soul-Swinging	84
That Prodigal Son!	87
Off To The Races!	89
The Ten Commandments In The Classroom	92
PART THREE ~ FOREGROUND	**95**
Emerging From The Galatian Gloom	97
Liberty	99
• *The Mission Statement*	*99*
Standing Firm	101
Our Calling	102
Liberty And Love Fulfil The Law	103
PART FOUR ~ TAKING GROUND	**105**
And The Galatians Rejoice!	107
Love	109
The Too-Hard Basket	111
• *On A Personal Note*	*113*
The Sample Basket	115
The Fruit Of The Spirit	118
A Creation Principle Or Law?	120
Legalism, Lawlessness Or Love On Our Roads?	121
The Primary Concept	124
'Breathing In The Spirit'	126
The Everyday Tasks	128
Holy Spirit Awareness	131
The 'Tree Of The Knowledge Of Walking In The Spirit'?	133
Law Or Expedience?	135
The Unveiled Face	137
The Wise Galatians	138
References	143
Afterword	149
Acknowledgments	151
About The Author	153

Also by Geoffrey Gay

LostRalia (Ark House Press)

An anachronistic allegorical narrative poem in the epic tradition

For our ten grandchildren and their future
families ~ God Willing ~ our legacy.

Also in memory of a 'very distant relative',
John Gay from County Devon in England,
whose infamous play *The Beggar's Opera* (1728)
was a veiled study in legalism and lawlessness.

*"Now, if you are led by spirit,
you are not still under law."*

Galatians 5:18
(Concordant Literal New Testament)

*"For whoever are being led by God's Spirit,
these are sons of God."*

Romans 8:14
(Concordant Literal New Testament)

A Quick Note About Usage

When referring to the writer of the letter to the Galatian church and others, I shall use a number of different titles. Christians from more traditional churches may prefer St Paul, others the apostle Paul, others brother Paul and yet others may prefer Paul by itself. I apologise to all of you by announcing that I shall use all of these honorifics to please every single one of you!

PART ONE

~

BACKGROUND

FOOLISH GALATIANS ANONYMOUS

"Hello everyone! My name is Geoff –
and I am a **FOOLISH GALATIAN**.
It's now been three weeks since my last terrible choice."
(*Millions applauding.*) "Hi Geoff !!!! Welcome, brother. Take a seat."

Most of us are aware of the confessional benefits of *Alcoholics Anonymous* and, not to make light of this highly respected organisation, there is sure to be a Chocoholics Anonymous somewhere on our planet. Could there be a Foolish Galatians Anonymous out there as well for the penitent glutton who has been overindulging on the tasty but destructive fruit of the Tree of the Knowledge of Good and Evil? This brief study provides signposts as to where and how this can happen.

Who then is a 'foolish Galatian'? For those who may not be familiar with some biblical terms, this quote from the apostle Paul's letter to a regional gathering of Christians throughout ancient Galatia, in what is now central modern Turkiye, could be of help:

"*O foolish Galatians! Who bewitches you, before whose eyes Jesus Christ was graphically crucified? This only I want to learn from you: Did you get the spirit by works of law or by the hearing of faith? So foolish are you? Undertaking in spirit, are you now being completed in flesh?*" (Galatians 3: 1-3; Con Lit NT)

According to this passage, a foolish Galatian is a person who has received the Holy Spirit by the 'hearing of faith', but then tries to complete the process towards sanctification that Christ began in them in their own flesh life; their own efforts; or 'the works of law'. This book will examine what 'their own efforts', or 'the works of law' means; as well as provide a biblical context for being made complete by and/or in the Holy Spirit.

Along this way we shall examine the life-giving words that St Paul used to convince the Galatian Christians of a better way; to lead them away from foolish perceptions and guide them into divine wisdom. Accompany me on this narrow road that can lead us to a greater appreciation of five concepts, either stated or implied, in the Galatian letter starting with the letter **L** (our Learner's plates so to speak):

LAW; LEGALISM; LICENCE (LAWLESSNESS); LIBERTY and LOVE.

How many Foolish Galatians Anonymous members out there are willing to hop on board and travel down this road with me?

'MISSION DRIFT' IN ASIA MINOR

It was the young man with the sweaty brow and hardened feet who made his way into the ancient town of Pisidian Antioch in the shadow of snowy mountain ranges to deliver an important missive. The messenger was the last of many who had relayed this scroll through various towns and villages along well-paved Roman roads; the scroll penned with personal difficulties by a certain persuasive, bold and balding Hellenic Jew who had been through these parts in recent times.

The messenger knew whither it must be delivered, and he was looking forward to his little reward when he handed it over to the elders of that small yet expanding gathering on the outskirts of the town. Entering a curtained portal, Suleyman made his way through a series of interior taverns and stalls; finally gathering his breath at the rear of a congregation of so-called 'believers,' a new sect that had emerged from the desert sands to the south-east and taken root throughout the Galatian region in central Asia Minor.

He gingerly approached whom he knew to be the local leader of the elders and revealed the parchment from the folds of his tattered robe.

"Ahh, the letter at last!" exclaimed the elder. "We have been expecting this one from our brother Paul. A coin for the young man and lead him yonder to sup with us. But now let us gather together and unwind this scroll..."

"What does it say, dear brother?" The others were eager for any news or teachings from afar. As the believers took their places in a semi-circle around

him, the elder read aloud Paul's customary introduction; praising His Lord and Saviour who had delivered them from their sins and the present evil age.

Suddenly the elder stopped reading; a tear now streaming down his bearded cheek. "What is it, dear brother? What is wrong?" the others pleaded.

The elder read on, trying to imitate Paul's forthright manner, but in his own faltering speech:

"I marvel that you are turning away so soon from Him who called you in the grace of Christ, to a different gospel, which is not another; but there are some who trouble you and want to pervert the gospel of Christ."

The elder paused, for the words were too bitter to absorb all at once. He looked up from the scroll. His brothers and sisters in the faith were eerily silent, rocked by the rebuke they had all just received. It was as if their beloved Paul had sucked the very wind out of their sails. The doldrums had set in; only to be relieved gradually by the teaching that followed in the remainder of the missive.

We shall leave our ancient *ecclesia* there for the time being as we discover a little more about the sub-heading above.

THE ORIGINAL DRIFT

In their 2014 book, **Mission Drift**[1] (Greer and Horst 2014), Peter Greer and Chris Horst brilliantly describe how easy it is for faith-based institutions to veer off from their original mission. In their book, the focus is on modern Christian institutions; the same principle operating for all types of companies worldwide. Even though they offer unparalleled, relevant and up-to-date advice for the modern Christian business owner, college principal or church pastor, they tend not to write much about mission drift in the history of the Christian church itself; intentionally no doubt.

One of the earliest instances of 'mission drift' in the Christian church was the one described above in the collective churches of the region of Galatia; now part of modern-day Türkiye. Historically this was a region occupied by northern ethnic Galatians who were considered to be related to the Celts and Gauls. There has also been reference to southern Galatians who had been occupied by the Roman empire. Most scholars believe that St Paul was writing to the latter as a result of Paul and Barnabas's first missionary journey (Harrison et al. 2015 p. 2136)[2]. In the context of the letter, it is implied that most of the Galatian believers in that region were part of the Jewish diaspora.

So why was the mission drift in Galatia so swift and so well-defined, as pointed out to the Galatians reading more of this letter; albeit to their chagrin?

> *"O foolish Galatians ………. Having begun in the Spirit, are you now being made perfect by the flesh?" (Gal. 3: 1 – 3; NKJV)*

What an outburst by our brother Paul! No wonder the description of the congregation had them looking like stunned mullets. Paul does not hesitate here; he jumps right in with the swiftness of a surgeon in an OR! How far from the original mission had the Galatians drifted, how long had it taken and what lessons might there be for us almost two thousand years later? We know that St Paul must have written this urgent letter before the council of Jerusalem in 49 or 50 AD and obviously after the first missionary journey in 48 AD. The drift wasn't prolonged – one or two years at the most. Before you know it, without realising it, you're losing sight of the shoreline without a sail!

It is one thing to recognise that we have drifted, but what exactly have we drifted from? If we have drifted from the mission, what was that original mission? If we have drifted from the gospel, what was that original gospel?

Answering these questions requires us to know what the actual Christian mission is. It is not enough to just make disciples – that constitutes only half of the mission, as any religious group or school of philosophy can also be doing the very same thing. (Let's not forget that the word 'disciple' derives from the Latin *discipulus* which means a *student follower* or *apprentice*, from which we then arrive at the word 'discipline' - it is not the other way around. The disciplines of the subject matter follow the teachings of the matter.)

Doesn't our Lord Jesus Himself command us to go into all the world and make disciples, as in Matthew 28 and verse 19? He does; and it is extremely important indeed. Yet He goes on to say in verse 20: "… teaching them to observe all things that I have commanded you; …".

This is the distinctive! This now completes the picture. We need to know what distinguishes Christian discipleship from all those other 'discipleships'. We need to know WHAT exactly is being taught. Doctrine is important as our actions always demonstrate either what we have been taught, or what we have taught ourselves. Our actions express and/or betray what we **really** believe or are disposed to. I confess to having learnt this many times over in embarrassing and humiliating ways.

By knowing this we shall obtain an understanding of how we fulfil the mission; otherwise, we shall fall into the same "foolish Galatian" roundabout, and somehow mistake THAT for the mission and its consequent discipleship programs, of which there have been legion over the last two thousand years.

We need to understand that the revelation given to the apostle Paul, the Pauline Revelation, is an integral part of the gospel teaching to which Jesus referred in Matthew 28. He already knew that when He instructed us to observe all things that He had commanded us to do. We are not only talking about Paul here, but Peter, James and John. What the Holy Spirit has taught us through these amazing brothers in Christ is the same as hearing it straight from the lips of Jesus Himself (which are quite often rendered in red ink in many Bible versions, but not throughout the NT epistles – for which there must have been a terrible shortage of cochineal).

In order to unravel these teachings in the context of this book, let us be as bold as Paul, or even Martin Luther, as we figuratively nail a **thesis** on the door of our hearts.

THESIS: The purpose of law in the grace dispensation under Christ's New Agreement (Covenant) is to return us to 'being led by God's Holy Spirit' as soon as possible. The 'work of law' is to make way for the 'hearing of faith'.

'THE MAN ON THE MIDDLE CROSS'

If you are a social-media participant, and very few of us are not, you may have come across a post featuring the Rev. Alistair Begg, entitled *The Man on the Middle Cross Said I Can Come*. In his delightful Scottish accent, and with humour and great conviction, Rev. Begg explains that the only reason the thief next to Jesus was able to join Him in paradise was because of his acceptance of Christ's declaration over him: *"Verily, to you am I saying today, with Me shall you be in paradise."* (Luke 23:43 Con Lit NT*)*. And effectively for the thief: *"He believed and it was accounted to him as righteousness."* (Romans 4:22 NKJV).

According to Begg, the thief had never been to a Bible study; had never gotten baptised; had never been a church member; and I am sure you can add to this list as Rev. Begg had begun to do. Yet the thief was able to explain why he was patiently and inexplicably waiting to be ushered into glory: *"The Man on the middle cross said I can come."* (Begg, 2021) [3]

Now fortunately for the vast majority of those of us who have placed our lives in Christ's Hands, we were not marched out to the back of the church building and summarily executed upon hearing the words: "Thank you up the back there; I see that hand!"; (albeit, seriously and tragically we are hearing more and more these days about the persecution and murders of Christians new and old around the world on a daily basis).

For most Christians, we must live out our lives in a way that was not required of the thief next to Jesus. For that man, there were only a few hours left; being literally immobile unto death. For us, we have whole lives to live, be that comparatively brief or extended. Therefore, we need to know how to live out this life of grace gifted by our Lord and Saviour. This is where the teaching of the apostle Paul to the Galatians complements the teachings that Jesus alluded to in Matthew 28:20. It is not separate from them!

DRIVING INSTRUCTIONS

To help us take advantage of those teachings, we shall commandeer the metaphor of driving a car – remember those Learner's plates? Each of the next five **L** plates will be the capital letter that begins a concept, as mentioned above.

The aim is to enable you to drive from one concept to the next. Do not worry about the **L** plates with what this might imply about *your* 'driving'; as Christians we are always learning new perspectives on God's Word….. even as I am writing this book!

Another aid that will be used is the table displayed below, entitled:

The **ASPIRANT BELIEVER**.

The shades in the table represent what would normally be traffic light colours:

RED	**STOP! U-TURN IMMEDIATELY.** It would be wise to avoid these roads.
AMBER	**BE PREPARED to STOP** and **RECOGNISE the ROAD SIGNS ...;**
GREEN	**PROCEED WITH JESUS.**

DRIVING INSTRUCTIONS

This table will guide us on our journey, but be prepared for a few little detours, roadblocks and rest areas along the way.

Are you ready? **Fasten your seat belts!**

The ASPIRANT BELIEVER

	The PENDULUM of the SOUL (swinging through the vast spectrum of human experiences in thought, word and deed)	
	(The TREE of the KNOWLEDGE of GOOD and EVIL - Gen. 2:17)	
LAW	Gal. 3:19, 23 - 26; 4:1-3 Rom. 7:12	our 'protector' and 'tutor' (guardian and steward) until faith (Christ) came!"
LEGALISM	Gal. 5:1, 13, 18; Matt. 23:24 Luke 15: 11 - 32	"under the law": a strict adherence to the letter of the law; is most often a mentality – a "yoke of bondage" – our own law! "straining at gnats"; elder son's flesh.
LICENCE (Lawlessness)	Gal. 5:13, Gal. 5:19 – 21; Matt. 23: 24 Luke 15: 11 - 32	above the law: giving ourselves permission to do whatever we want to do; "swallowing camels"; younger son's flesh.
	The PLUMB LINE of the HOLY SPIRIT (steadfast vertical orientation and focus on Christ) (The TREE of LIFE) Gen. 3: 22 -23	
LIBERTY / LED by the SPIRIT	Gal. 5:1,13-14, Gal. 5:18; 2 Cor. 3: 17; Rom. 8:14; 6:14	"neither under nor above law": learning the spirit of the law; practising the presence of the spirit; mature 'sonship'.
LOVE	Gal. 5:13-14 Gal. 6: 2	"fulfils the law": serving one another in love.

© Geoffrey Raymond Gay, 2025

PART TWO

~

SHAKY GROUND

MEANWHILE, BACK IN TURKIYE .....

Young Suleyman was greedily absorbed in scoffing down his little loaf of bread and the cup of water that had been part of his reward when he noticed that the chamber in which the 'believers' were meeting had become deathly quiet. He looked up from his introversion and saw several men with their hands upon the shoulders of others and some women who were comforting their companions. An atmosphere of melancholy had descended upon the room.

"Has a loved one died?" thought the youth, who was unused to seeing such genuine affection on display. He now began to take notice of what was being said, his attention captured as his eating came to an abrupt end.

"My dear brothers and sisters," continued the elder, after wiping away his initial tear. "There is much more to read here, and we must go on." Paul's rebuke now changed into a narrative: how he had become an apostle to the gentiles and his meetings with the original apostles who had talked and walked with Jesus Himself; how he had actually stood toe-to-toe with a man named Cephas and rebuked him for not standing up for Paul's message when surrounded by his own countrymen.

And then came a rebuke which the elder could hardly pass through his quivering lips: *"O foolish Galatians! Who bewitches you, before whose eyes Jesus Christ was graphically crucified? This only I want to learn from you: Did you get the spirit by works of law or by the hearing of faith? So foolish are you? Undertaking in spirit, are you now being completed in flesh?"*

The rest of the words from the elder were hard to capture, for Suleyman could hear weeping from some of the assembled believers. Although he wasn't sure what the elder was alluding to, he felt like he himself had been slapped in the face for just being a native Galatian. Who would be rude enough to insult these people in their very own dwellings!

He returned his attention to the elder who by this time had taken a few very deep breaths, with encouragement from his brethren, and continued to verbalise Paul's explanation of righteousness and faith and something about why we had to have law. These Jewish Galatians were really passionate about their faith, although they were suddenly taken aback when the elder pointed out Paul's reminder that in Christ there are no longer any Jews or Greeks. What is this Christ doing to these people that is destroying those now occupying Galatia, thought Suleyman with concern now written all over his face? He wasn't really sure about the meaning behind what was said, but he heard another man's name entering the story – Abraham. Yes, he thought that he had heard of this ancient name somewhere before, but his interest was piqued when the elder began to read the next section of the letter concerning Abraham's two sons. One was named, but the other one was not. The one that was not named was the son of his maid, but the named one, Isaac, was born of his wife and seemed to be the favoured one.

But wait, did he not previously hear about another son who was sent from God Himself, born under the law to set free others who were also under the law? This was all very confusing to young Suleyman, and he hoped that he could hear more about this one sent from God. Was that one Isaac or someone else whose name had escaped him?

Suleyman's eyes were beginning to close with weariness, although something was stirring in his heart; a strange attraction that drew him in further to the reading.

...to be continued.

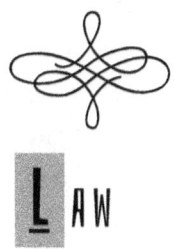

Law

KEY SCRIPTURE
"Now, if you are led by spirit,
you are not still under law."
Galatians 5:18 (Con Lit NT)

GETTING THE RIGHT ANSWER!

You may have heard this saying:

"If you want the right answer, ask the right question!"

How many of us have the wisdom to be able to ask the right questions when it comes to reading and understanding the Word of God? To me, being able to do this is a divine revelation in itself. It is a divine revelation that leads to more divine revelation.

When I first said "Yes to Jesus" or the equivalent thereof back in 1974, there was, among other things going on at the time, a huge theological debate about law versus grace (or faith). I was totally wrapped up in this argument because most of the new denominations in those days were preaching against the law as if it were our enemy; a thing to be despised; looked down upon; criticised; and ridiculed (especially those people who belonged to those denominations who appeared to us to be lawful!) This, of course, was never befitting a fruitful Christian.

So, in true Berean style (Acts 17:10-15), I decided to find out for myself what the big fuss was all about. As a young Christian I really wanted to know the 'mechanics' of doctrines and how these concepts actually worked; albeit that approach certainly didn't stop me from getting tied up in mental and emotional knots! After a few years I prayed specifically about *this* challenge. As a reply, God gave me a question to ask; (you might be surprised how many people and doctrines are not understood simply because we do not ask the right questions).

So I prayed something like this: "Dear Father, could you please show me some verses that will help me understand law, and how it fits in with what I think I know so far about our Christian walk? In Jesus's name, amen." That was a loaded question, with God supplying a loaded answer!

Over time my attention was turned towards what I believe to be one of the most understated books in the Bible: **The Epistle of Paul the Apostle to the Galatians**, to give it its New King James Version title. This letter is full of references to law, and, as I discovered, more concepts beginning with the letter **L**. And who better to explain what law is about, but the apostle Paul himself!

PERRY MASON IN SANDALS

Baby-boomers may well remember Raymond Burr's portrayal of the infallible American lawyer, Perry Mason; not the modern-day take on the character; the one back in the days when we only had monochrome televisions in Australia. Burr's character was flawless, as he would cut through tricky cases to uncover the truth, the whole truth and nothing but the truth, so helped him God.

Back in the first century *anno Domini (AD – in the year of the Lord)* the apostle Paul was the Perry Mason of the Middle East. As a Pharisee, he would have been well-versed in the law of his people. In fact, he was the expert in law in the Roman province of Judea. St Paul's own expression was 'Pharisee of the Pharisees' used in the context of a public stoush with the Sadducees (Acts 23:6). He later backed this up with a 'fleshy' boast: "...concerning law, a Pharisee;…" (Phil. 3:5). Effectively, the law was embedded in brother Paul through both birth and profession.

Yet Paul was more than just this. According to Thomas Smith, *'He was a tri-part person - a Jew (from the tribe of Benjamin and a member of the Pharisee movement), a Roman citizen raised in a Hellenised (Greek) culture, and a disciple of his Resurrected Rabbi, Jesus."* (Smith, 2008 [4]). In a previous article he wrote: *'Paul spoke and wrote in Greek, and was not unfamiliar with other facets of Greek culture. He knew their philosophers and poets (Acts 18:19-32), and his letters follow classical Greek style and etiquette. Part of this is due to his place of origin - Tarsus. Of it, Paul reminds us it was "no mean city" (Acts 21:39), in other words, it was not some backwater village. One ancient writer called Tarsus a "little Athens" of learning. St. Paul wisely took what was good and valuable in that culture, incorporated it into his Jewish faith, and used it as a springboard to discuss the Resurrection in the heart of Athens.'* (Smith, 2008 [5]). If Tertullian's disciples in the third century AD were looking for an answer to Tertullian's question: *"What has Athens to do with Jerusalem?"*[6], they may well have found it in the historic figure of Paul himself.

What does this mean for this little thesis? When the apostle Paul teaches us about law, it would be foolish of us not to take notes!

DEFINING LAW

Now this is where I am going to get into trouble with many legal eagles sitting in their chambers (and some teachers in churches), so we had better drive carefully here! For the purpose of this discourse, I shall avoid one particular meaning of the word 'law' which is used as a principle of science; e.g. The Law of the Conservation of Mass-Energy (which, let's face it, is all about eternity anyway. NB: In the universality of God's Creation, it would not be wise to separate anything, but for this brief study, we shall go where angels fear to tread!). There are other types of law that come under the general heading of 'urban law', like the Law of Unintended Consequences (anon.) and Murphy's Law (Murphy?), but I shall leave those alone too so I don't get too entangled in them myself whilst writing this essay.

Initially, we shall define law in terms related to legal matters. Customarily, like all good students preparing for a debate, we shall firstly visit the dictionary. Here is the number **1a** definition of law (Moore et al., 2001, p620) [7]:

n. rule enacted or customary in a community and recognised as commanding or forbidding certain actions.

Following this are ten more definitions including, but not limited to: *the body of law, law and order, social systems, binding force, jurisprudence, courts, Aboriginal law* etc., mostly relating directly back to the original definition.

Many other terms are used, both legally and academically, to represent law. We can use terms such as rules, regulations, statutes, by-laws, ordinances, acts, legislation, constitutions, enactments, mandates, boundaries, precepts; plus many terms that are related to these. Each one of these terms are used in different contexts and for different purposes. For all their apparent differences, what would bind these terms together under one word – law?

LAW AS COMPULSION

As finicky as we may get legally with the differences between the terms used above, they all have one thing in common: the **ELEMENT** of **COMPULSION**. There is no doubt that, except for mitigating evidence or circumstances offered in a court of law, the directions behind *all* of these different synonyms of law **MUST BE OBEYED**! *Adherence is compulsory*, as there is a raft of punishments for recalcitrants lined up for their efficacious reformation.

A law is something **WE EITHER HAVE TO DO** or **NOT DO**!

If you have to do it, it is compulsory. If you are not allowed to do it, that is also compulsory. In another word, it is law. It doesn't matter what label you put on them, they still all have that same fundamental function.

Laws usually reflect the moral climate of the day in any society or group, as morals are very simply what we either believe we should do or not do generally or in any given situation. In the latter case, sometimes the word **ethics** is bandied about in relevant contexts.

In our society we have a legal foundation called 'The Rule of Law', which, according to the Australian Constitution Centre, is *'the idea that every person is subject to the laws of the land regardless of their status.*[8] (ACC, 2024). Furthermore: *"It is also the idea that you cannot be punished or have your rights affected other than in accordance with a law, and only after a breach *of the law has been established in a court of law."* (ibid.) Consequently, even in our own country, we are ALL regarded as 'under law'! We shall revisit this concept in a later section.

FURTHER INSIGHTS?

I am reminded of a line that our leading pastor at Life Church in Brisbane once used to describe law: *"Law only deals with action."* (Blight [9], 2023) By this he was referring to the transformative nature of our relationship with Christ: that he has made us a new creature (Gal. 6:16, 2 Corinthians 5:17). For Pastor Blight then, law only deals with compliance, as according to Romans 12:2, *"God transforms us into a new person by changing the way we think."* Being a *"new creation is not just modified behaviour."*

Therefore one could add that being merely compliance, law is transactional in nature; it has consequences.

Now let's try a slightly different tack with a variation on the definition of law:

Law is an expression or reflection of what we would naturally be and do walking with Jesus in the first place. It became transactional and binding rather than relational and loving.

For a reminder of 'the first place', turn to Genesis and read chapters 2 and 3.

THREE TYPES OF LAW

There are a few types of **LAW** that we shall cover here to allay any confusion about its concept and purpose. Theologians and lawyers will no doubt have a much longer list but for the purpose of our study these shall be offered.

The **first** type of law that we're dealing with here, especially relevant to Christians, is Old Testament or Judaic law (the Tanakh – the 'Bible' at the time of Jesus). No doubt Paul was generally pointing to this law when he addressed the Galatians, and others. He specifically mentioned the ritual of circumcision as a point of contention (Gal. 5: 2-12). Many of the Galatian Christians were Jews, following the precepts of Judaism (which in future discussions will be my reference point for this type of law, rather than the identification of Jews as an ethnic group). The general term of 'moral law' is included under Old Testament law, with many maintaining that this type of law continues in its original form. This is true up to a point, when the nature of being led by His Spirit is understood.

Also, many Christians believe that Paul was only referring to 'ceremonial' law in this particular letter. Interestingly, in a literal translation of Galatians in chapter 5 verse 18, Paul uses the word 'law' without a preposition which would normally have given a more specific definition (Con Lit NT). Many languages like ancient Greek, English and Latin-based languages, such as Spanish and French, do use them; whereas languages like Latin itself, Russian

THREE TYPES OF LAW

and some northern English dialects do not! It may be that our brother Paul is hinting at the fact that all types of law are alluded to here; that when I obey the road rules, or just pay attention to my own spouse throughout our marriage, or obey a direct instruction from a police officer, I'm doing so from a higher motivation than just obeying transactional law generally. This is a key to our understanding of Galatians 5:18. For a more formal coverage of law and its biblical purpose, please refer to (Tait, 2023)[10].

For Aussies, and this also applies to everyone regardless of national jurisdiction, there are the laws of one's own country. For the Aussie Christian, some of our laws may coincide with values we still hold dear; others may not. Nevertheless, all modern-day Aussies are under our national laws, state laws and/or local government laws depending on where on this vast continent you live. These represent our **second** type of law.

The **third** type of law refers to **the ones we make up ourselves and either enshrine them in many different ways within various institutions or store them away in our own being to drag them out whenever we feel it necessary to do so.** We make them up **in our own heads!** This also applies to everyone; Christian or not. Some may even include 'natural law' under this heading. Whichever way we look at personal laws, as Darren Copland alludes to in his book *Killing the CEO* (Copland, 2025, p. 4)[11], they can so easily become **foundational beliefs**, even ones we acquire during our childhood. It's as if we were engraving our own laws on tablets of stone; seemingly divine to us but quite breakable in the long run.

[CONCERNING COMPULSION

The idea of compulsion is not new of course as the word is also used to describe aberrations in behaviour sourced from mental illness. Compulsive behaviour can lead one to an *"act based on ritual"* (Mayo Clinic, 2023) [12]. The rituals are often thematic in nature and they are habitual. I wonder how many of our compulsory, legalistic rituals are based on an unhealthy compartmentalised pseudo-Christian worldview that are merely thematic and habitual for its own sake; although I do not view times of communion in church, for example, as ritualistic or compulsive unless the original purpose is forgotten. Rf. First Corinthians 11:23-34. In passing, it's interesting that the non-Christian world itself sees compulsive ritualism as an unhealthy characteristic in any person whom a Christian would consider as a candidate for divine healing.

Back on the main road now.]

How then, from a spiritual point of view, did we get to this era of **compulsion**?

THE BEGINNING OF LAW

To make an exceedingly long story short, biblical law began as a way of keeping a whole nation unified and in line by making it known to them what they should do or not do; what the divine expectations were. This was done in the context of their deliverance from Egypt under Moses. Of course, this was not the first time nations had law. Most school students will have heard of the Hammurabi Code, for example, which served the Babylonians well for hundreds of years even before Moses himself turned up. And, obviously, there were many other legal codes in ancient times.

Yet when Adam and Eve were forbidden to return to the Garden to eat from the Tree of Life in Genesis 3:22 - an event I explore allegorically in my narrative poem *LostRalia* (Gay, 2019) [13] -, there was no stated law at that time. We even read this in Romans 5:13: *For until the law sin was in the world, but sin is not imputed when there is no law.* (NKJV) Death still naturally kicked in because of the 'original sin' according to Genesis 2:17, but there was no spiritual or national law enacted for God's Chosen until Exodus 20 with the giving of the Ten Commandments and the other 603 instructions.

It is interesting to note that when the apostle Paul refers to law, he includes Genesis as an example. In Galatians 4: 21 until the end of the chapter, he begins with: *Tell me, you who desire to be under the law, do you not hear the law?* Now at this stage, he does not launch into a description of the Ten Commandments. Rather, he continues with: *For it is written that Abraham had two sons: the one by a bondwoman, the other by a freewoman.* And the lesson goes on. He is not quoting from Exodus here; he is quoting from Genesis. So even though the law was the enacted instructions to the new nation of Israel *after* the exodus from Egypt, Paul, the lawyer, regarded everything *before* it as law as well. (Rf. Tait, 2023 [10] for Hebraic meanings.)

We read in Genesis how from Abraham's immediate family the Hebrew nation was birthed. At the time they travelled to Egypt to escape severe famine in Canaan, it is estimated that there were about seventy of them in Jacob's (Israel's) household. By the end of Israel's captivity in Egypt a few hundred years later, it is 'guesstimated' that there were anything up to two million of them (Ryken, 2023) [14]!

With a family household you would need relatively few customary rules (harking back to our dictionary definition). By the time you have reached two million people, you really do need a set of laws, or in this case, the 613 commandments of the Torah, to do several different things; not necessarily in the following order:

First, you need to be able to keep everyone from doing unseemly things. You do not want a sizeable number of people running around like yahoos simply because they are now out from under slavery's whip. Remember the Golden Calf in Exodus 32?

Second, you need a 'banner' under which everyone can unite and have common goals. Most importantly, the unity described in Psalm 133 and verse 1 would consequently bring forth the blessing – life forevermore, which one could interpret to also mean Yeshua, the Messiah, as in John chapter 14 and verse 6.

Third, you need to be able to fight for each other, and not against each other. Factions and schisms can happen so quickly. Just ask Cain and Abel!

Fourth, you need to move ahead as one, both spiritually and structurally – albeit extremely slowly in this case. What could have taken only eleven days took these people forty years to get to the promised land, so please don't complain about my little detours in this book!

Fifth, and most importantly, you need a focus – in this case – Jehovah God Himself. What were His first words to them through Moses in Exodus 20: 2? *I am the Lord your God, ….*". If those words do not get your attention, well ……

Significantly, the apostle Paul does not necessarily take my personal list to heart when he gives the **three major reasons** for law in Galatians (and other letters). These are not just applicable to **THE** law, but also to the principle behind law itself.

[IS GOD'S LAW FOREVER?

Before we plunge into the purposes of law in Galatians, let's try to settle this question whilst resting in His wisdom. Scriptures like Psalm 119: 89, 151-2, 160; Deuteronomy 7:9, 12:1 and First Chronicles 16:15 (Solberg, 2020) [15] seem to indicate that it is eternal. According to Prof. R L Solberg in his article *Is the Law of Moses Eternal?* (ibid.) the original biblical Hebrew words used for *eternal or everlasting* may have slightly different meanings according to context. I highly recommend you read this article, and especially the brutal comments responding to his thesis from both Judaists and Christians!

For the purpose of my thesis the timelessness or continuation of law is of little relevance, except for the one purpose I reiterate throughout this work. Why? Once faith came, we are no longer under a tutor or law (Galatians 3:25). Sure, the law, and law generally, is still here, but our goal is to raise the bar a level and start walking in His Spirit. The motivation returns to the walking that occurred back in the original paradise.

Refreshed? On our way again!]

COMMANDS - THE ULTIMATE LAWS AND PURPOSES?

In the terms that were used above to represent the many facets of law, I deliberately omitted the word 'command'; albeit not excluded in the dictionary definition. Logically, wouldn't this be included in my definitions? Normally yes, but admittedly I faced a possible misunderstood contradiction between Jesus giving commands to his disciples on one hand and Paul instructing a wider audience of disciples to be led by the Spirit; avoiding being under law. What then, if any, is the connection? My recourse was to dive back into the dictionary and biblical concordance.

A quick thumb through the *Analytical Concordance to the Holy Bible* (Young,1939) [16] revealed a number of different meanings for the words 'command' and 'commandment' depending on their exegetical context. Without going through all the Hebrew and Greek words used variously throughout the Old and New Testaments (which you can research yourselves), let's observe the diversity in meanings for the words 'command', 'commandment' and 'commander':

to say; lift up the voice; to speak; lead forth words; to arrange thoroughly; to give in charge; to put upon or over; to call to, urge on, command; to announce alongside of; to arrange, set in order; to announce; to set or give a reason; precept, thing set up; to be set up, receive a precept; taste, reason, law; to set throughout; a word; thing given, a law, judgement; statute; charge; the mouth.

Although the words 'command', 'law' and 'statute' are used as renderings in English, they are used sparingly in the NT, either to quote from the OT, as orders given to others during an act described or ironically by Paul when usually giving forceful instructions or advice to church elders (probably to get them back into being led by the Spirit again!).

The sense of the meanings given by Dr Young seem to indicate that God is setting up His Sovereignty in the hearts of believers. He is urging us, arranging things for us, setting things in order, giving us a taste (Cf. Psalm 34:8); setting Himself up as worthy to be trusted; establishing precepts in the very depths of our being.

Does this mean that we are now excusing ourselves from **OBEYING** God? Am I watering down or dumbing down the impact of the word so that I can excuse myself in my attitudes and actions? *"Certainly not!"* echoing Paul again. It means that our obedience to God is not based on legal transactions but on the awe He inspires in us in His Presence! **This is how we can obey God whilst walking in His Spirit.** The old adage *"your wish is my command"* comes quickly to mind here; although that sounds more like a line out of a fairy tale. Whatever proceeds from God's mouth is sure to get us on our bikes, especially if what comes out of His mouth is meant for other people's ears to bless and encourage them in some way!

Another saying I am reminded of is that *"leaders do not **demand** loyalty or trust, they **command** it"*. The subtlety of this English word 'command' is not lost on those who have been inspired in their own roles as leaders. One definition of this form of 'command' in our dictionaries is to *"4 deserve and get (...respect, etc.)"* (op.cit., pp 204, 205) [7]. Our obedience to God is, of course, more than just respect, but I tend to steer towards this definition of 'command' in relation to my walk with Him.

COMMANDS – THE ULTIMATE LAWS AND PURPOSES?

In this section I shall leave you with the meeting of the Roman centurion with Jesus in Matthew chapter 8 and verses 5 to 13 which you can read at your leisure. As you will note, the centurion's faith response to Jesus when requesting that his servant be healed was: *"For I also am a man under authority…"*. (v9). Jesus marvelled at this gentile's faith and healed his servant from afar. This story also indicates that a believer needs to be **UNDER AUTHORITY**, but not under law. What was significant here is the centurion's **heart posture**.

THE PURPOSE OF THE LAW ACCORDING TO PAUL IN GALATIANS

Once Paul has finished berating the Galatian Christians with an accusation of gullibility at the start of chapter 3, he gently yet firmly repositions his brothers and sisters in Christ with a reiteration of truth. You could call it 'Christianity 101', for this truth is the one from which we have 'mission drifted'[1] on and off for twenty centuries.

To help us arrive at the purposes of law, let's summarise Gal. 3: 10-18 in bullet point order:

- because we could not obey the whole law, but tried to, we were under a curse (v.10);
- no one is justified by the law; the just will live by faith (v. 11);
- the law is NOT from or of faith (v. 12);
- Christ has redeemed us from the curse of the law, having become the curse himself (apart from the reference to hanging on a cursed tree, the implication is that Christ became the embodiment of the law that was crucified as instructed in 2 Corinthians 5:21, thereby **fulfilling the law** from His prophetic obligations) (v.13);

- that the blessing that this generates would be for the gentiles as well as for the Jews. Through faith (not the law), we would receive the promise of the Spirit (v.14);
- with any agreement made between people, no one can negate it nor add to it (one implication: how much more binding is an agreement made by and with God!) (v. 15);
- well before the law was enacted with Moses, God made promises to Abraham and his Seed (Christ) which cannot be annulled or nullified (v.16, 17); and
- a promise cannot be enacted by law, but was heralded by the law (v.18, and ch. 4:21 et al)!

Having laid the foundation, St Paul now comes to the crux of the matter (pun intended as *crux* in Latin means the or a cross). In chapter 3:19 and onwards, he begins to clarify the three main purposes of law, and why it was given.

PURPOSE NUMBER ONE: Law was added **BECAUSE** of our **TRANSGRESSIONS** (Rf. Romans 3:20 and 1 Timothy 1:5-11). First, the law was added. Added to what? Added to God's expectations in the first place; refer to Romans 5:13. Then the law shows us what our transgressions (sin/s) look like, and what being led by His Spirit looks like, if we are ever in doubt! In verse 19 it is specifically pointed out that this purpose was there *"till the Seed should come to whom the promise was made...;"* (NKJV).

PURPOSE NUMBER TWO: the law kept us **UNDER GUARD**, preserved or kept for something about to happen. Something or someone was anticipated.

PURPOSE NUMBER THREE: the law was our **TUTOR**, bringing us to a specific point in time. I have often told my own school students over the years that there will come a time when they won't need us teachers anymore at this level. They will graduate to a new level that will require others to lead and guide them, and maybe they will have similar roles themselves. I will no longer be required! Facing one's own redundancy is always a sobering experience.

The tutor in ancient Rome was on many occasions a Greek scholar (most likely a slave) who taught the children, usually the boys of the household (depending on social status etc). When the boys had taken on the *toga virilis*, they would progress to a new level of education if so desired by their *paterfamilias*. The **TUTOR WOULD NO LONGER BE REQUIRED!**

> Let us repeat that one: the *tutor would no longer be required* -
> **ergo, the LAW would no longer be required!**
> *SELAH (or 'think on this!')* ...

Again, in chapter 4: 1-3, he states: *Now I say that the heir, as long as he is a child, does not differ at all from a slave, though he is master of all, but is under guardians and stewards until the time appointed by the father. Even so we, when we were children, were in bondage under the elements of the world. But when the fullness of the time had come* ...(NKJV). You can read the next few verses victoriously!

These three purposes, clarified by Paul, encapsulate the essence of the PURPOSE of the law.

The law brought us FROM SOMEWHAT - TO SOMEONE. In Gal. 3: 24, we read that *the law was our tutor to bring us to Christ, that we might be justified by faith*. A few verses before this, brother Paul asks, *Is the law then against the promises of God? Certainly not!* was his forthright answer. *For if there had been a law given which could have given life, truly righteousness would have been by the law. But the Scripture has confined all under sin, that the promise by faith in Jesus Christ might be given to those who believe.* (verses 21 and 22)

[CONCERNING THE WORD 'UNDER'

As an aside, isn't it interesting that there are three translated phrases with the same preposition – **under** - as in "under sin", "under the elements" and "under law"? Then there is 'under authority' which shall be dealt with soon. *Selah,* then **drive off.**]

According to the apostle Paul and the sacrifice of Christ Himself, the law wasn't enough to guarantee salvation.

The key point here, and this is the point of this whole book, is that **THE PURPOSE of the LAW (and LAW generally) IS TO BRING US OUT FROM UNDER ITSELF !** It is designed as a SAFETY NET for EITHER YOURSELF AND/OR OTHERS. Yet we are **not meant to remain on the safety net.** We are meant to leave the safety net and "come to faith" (Christ). The old Latin injunction *cessante ratione legis cessat ipsa lex* - *"when the reason for the law ceases, the law itself ceases"* – could be invoked here, except for one significant point. Law, as a principle of God's Creation, still has a purpose.

THE GALATIAN COROLLARIES

As noted above, our key scripture is Galatians 5:18.

> *Now if you are led by Spirit,*
> *you are not still under law. (Con Lit NT)*

Hidden within this scripture rests what is called a **corollary**.

A **corollary** is "**1** a proposition that follows from one already proved" and/or a "**2** (often foll. by *of*) natural consequence or result." (op. cit., p235) [7]

Galatians 5:18, plus its partner in verse 16, form the most important corollaries in the whole of God's Word; corollaries that, when ignored, have unwittingly led to misunderstandings, much controversy and unnecessary pathways!

The corollary is this:
(my words and emphases now, based on verse 18 in the Con Lit NT!):
Now, if you are NOT led by Spirit,
you ARE still under law!
- and for verse 16:

..., Walk NOT in spirit, and you should under circumstances be consummating the lust of the flesh. (based on Con Lit NT)

This is a principle of God's Creation for ALL humans. This is why we have rules for students at school. In Christian school settings, for example, we would dearly like to think that ALL of our children are walking in the Spirit, but, alas, not all are! Rules, as law, are a reminder to students in Christian schools (or anywhere for that matter) that we have an opportunity to resume walking in the Spirit. The relevant rule is a guard for others, and a tutor to the student, to come back to Christ.

Let's not forget the Christian school staff either. We also have rules, under which we abide, should we not choose to be walking in the Spirit. I'm so grateful that I was employed by Christian schools whose principals were continually encouraging us to walk in the Holy Spirit, and to empower our students to do likewise.

**The more walking around in the Holy Spirit there is,
the less LAW we need to deal with
(and consequently 'crime and punishment',
with acknowledgements to Dostoevsky and Kohlberg).**

This principle applies to being a teacher, a student, a boss, a worker, a giver, a recipient – yes, whoever and whatever.

The principle, the **key to our Christian lives**, is simple, but difficult in ourselves to actualise (Rf. Romans ch. 7):

**Implied in my little thesis is that the whole aim of
Christian theology with the actualisation of that theology
is to REVERSE the Galatian COROLLARIES!**

The PURPOSE of LAW generally or THE LAW, the Tanakh (Hebrew Bible in Jesus' time), is to use it to get us back to WALKING in the SPIRIT, hopefully in a nanosecond! This could also be referred to as repentence.

Alas, for some people, this may take as long as a jail sentence, even for Christians who were not led by the Holy Spirit in a particular aspect of their lives. This is a CREATION PRINCIPLE from which none of us can escape; and who would want to should you have a relationship with Christ?

This is why faith (Christ) came! We are **NOT MEANT** to **LIVE 'UNDER LAW'**, but to **WALK in or be LED by HIS SPIRIT** (Galatians 5:18). This, by the way, is what Jesus is teaching us to do (Matt. 28:20), using the passion and legal experience of the apostle Paul to drive home the revelation!

Hence, the Letter to the Galatians!

THE GALATIAN COROLLARIES

[PUNISHMENT 'UNDER LAW'

The most complex aspect for me whilst meditating on the concept of law is the reality of choosing punishments for breaking law, especially for Christians erring on the unacceptable side of moral 'law'. In this grace dispensation, and especially in the year 2025, do we take an adulterous couple to the outskirts of the town and stone them to death (Rf. John 8:4,5) or burn witches at the stake as has happened even in the last few hundred years? Just contemplating these types of punishments had me losing lots of sleep over the years because the dilemma comes from a New Testament scripture itself. If I'm not walking in His Spirit and am now under law, what does that mean now in the context of possible punishments for me according to the letter written by James, the half brother of Jesus, when he states: *"For whoever shall keep the whole law and yet stumble in one* point (sic), *he is guilty of all. For He who said,* 'Do not commit adultery,' *also said,* 'Do not murder.' *Now if you do not commit adultery, but you do murder, you have become a transgressor of the law."* (James chapter 2 verses 10, 11 NKJV)

The last person in Australia to be hanged for murder was Ronald Ryan on exactly this date as I type - February 3rd 1967, only 58 years ago! (AG Staff, 2024) [17]. I can still remember the mug shots of Ryan and his accomplice, Peter Walker, staring at us all from the front page of Melbourne's afternoon papers. They had escaped from jail at Christmastime in 1965 and with me only 9 years old at the time and staying with my grandparents in a Melbourne suburb, I recall being scared to death while they were still on the run; yet eventually strangely horrified at the thought of Ryan being executed over a year later. Even at that young age, I felt empathetic towards Ryan, yet at the same time felt that justice had been done for the guard at HM Prison Pentridge who had been shot and killed when Ryan and Walker were escaping; and for the guard's family. It is a controversial issue all over the globe; and there is sure to be a variety of perspectives from this readership.

So the dilemma staring us in the face even now is: if a law has been broken, under which jurisdiction should a person be punished, if at all? Normally we would refer to the legislation of our federal or state governments here in Australia or in whichever jurisdiction you happen to live. Do we refer to 'spiritual' law as a form of jurisdiction, given that during much of history the distinction between 'spiritual' law and statute law has been very thin indeed; hence the modern penchant for separation of church and state? I'm beginning to sink in very murky waters here indeed, and am very thankful for my own pathetic preservation that crimes in my state jurisdiction are treated with relevant leniency compared to that of, say, the Holy Roman Empire or even the Ottoman Empire (you choose your own historical context here).

My only answer to this dilemma is that I remain a man 'under authority', and that I should humbly accept any punishment coming my way should I have criminally erred in some way in the particular jurisdiction I find myself; even for challenging any government decree forbidding the private or public practice of my faith. (By the way, you may like to check out recent stories from the UK about folk being fined for 'mindful praying' for women and their unborn babies who entered abortion clinics nearby. And this in my own indigenous country! I'm still reeling from this news.)

As to moral law, as included in the Torah and parts of the NT, I doubt whether anyone in our modern church is going to punish one in exactly the same way for a sin not punishable by the courts; albeit a few congregants might be heavily tempted to drag one out into the town square and throw rotten vegies at one whilst one is in the stocks. There will no doubt be ecclesiastical consequences, but usually accompanied with grace and mercy, one hopes! Suffice to say, the principal of legally-based punishment still

exists; although I do thank our Lord Jesus for the amazing way he dealt with the adulterous woman in John chapter 8. Hope has always been an integral part of His love for us. *Selah.*
Roadblock lifted – continue journey.]

[SO SOON! CONCERNING BOUNDARIES

Now what about **BOUNDARIES**? Aren't they just an acceptable way of dealing with everyday behavioural issues, like keeping your toddler from running out onto the street; or having your seventeen year old opening up that squeaky front gate by well before 1:00 am; or even setting up 'boundaries' within relationships?

Are boundaries laws; some form of legalism? Aren't they just rules that stop people from doing what they're not supposed to do? Haven't Christian churches fully adopted the concept of boundaries and incorporated that into their teachings in the last thirty or so years?

Yes they are and yes they have, but for one reason and one reason only. Often those who promote this concept still don't understand that the purpose of law is to ultimately background itself. Not obliterate itself; albeit, to have it standing by in case!

In February 1994, a popular article was written by Dr Sheila Pritchard entitled: ***Digging Wells or Building Fences*** (Shalom House of Prayer, 2017) [18]. This article tells the story of a rural property in Australia that had not built fences to keep its livestock within the property's boundary. There were many reasons for this, no doubt the size of the property being a prohibitive factor. Instead, they provided wells around the centre of the property as an incentive for the livestock to come and drink from its waters. Notwithstanding the many points listed in this recommended article, some focusing on the theme of this book, the upshot of the story from a Christian point of view is that if access to God's Holy Spirit is provided, then His children are not going to stray into unsanctioned territory.

This is a great illustration, but like most metaphors, even mine, it has limitations. Despite a few metaphorical references in the Bible to humans being sheep, goats or cattle with certain characteristics (usually stupid ones), the reality is that we humans are not livestock! We have been uniquely made in the image of God Himself! Usually, unless they are feeling threatened or hungry or in pain, animals will just follow their God-given instincts. There are some psychologists who will have us believe exactly the same about ourselves – tinkling bells or not.

Humans on the other hand spend their days making choices. We were given our own free will in the Garden of Eden, and that has not changed! We have our own agendas, and we can choose to either be led by the Spirit, be bound by law or to do our own thing. We are not robots nor are we Pavlov's dogs. We do respond in certain ways to stimuli but depending on whether we are talking about the central nervous system or the autonomic nervous system, we can generally control our choices. My experience as a schoolteacher spanning over forty years (mainly in various types of Christian schooling) has taught me that there are a certain number of students who arrive at school with their own agenda: deliberately failing to wear their school uniforms properly if their school requires such; going out of their way to be disruptive; seeking personal attention at the expense of others; generally wanting to do their own thing. With respect to what psychologists may diagnose for some of these children, and taking into account a few students who are genuinely suffering from poor domestic situations or just plain boredom, let's instead use a Biblical concept to describe the behavior stemming from deliberately alternative agendas – **LICENCE** or **LAWLESSNESS**. This concept will be dealt with in a following section, but suffice to say for the brief study of **boundaries**, we need those 'fences' to stop us from hurting ourselves and others and to guide our behaviours despite the fact that there is a 'well' provided for us. What is in fact a boundary is nothing less than law. Remember, law is something we have to do or not do. A boundary fence, realistically and metaphorically, stops us from wandering and keeps other undesirables out. (Indeed, boundaries may not only be for us; they may also be for Satan. He is under law. He is taking licence. He is the ultimate soul-swinger!)

Of course most of us desire to drink from the well, but nobody can be forced to do that. That is something we, as humans, will eventually want to do. Yes, we can be drawn by the Holy Spirit, but that usually happens when we have an "ear to hear" (Rf. Revelation 2:7)

In the meantime, the boundary fence, law, exists to protect and teach (Gal. 3:19) and to lead us back to Christ (the well) and being led by His Spirit. Ideally this needs to take place in a nanosecond, but sometimes it takes a little longer, especially if that process is taking place in a jail cell for twenty years.

Roadblock lifted.]

LAW	Gal. 3:19, 23 -26; 4: 1-3.	our 'protector' and 'tutor' (guardian and steward) until faith (Christ) came!

© Geoffrey Raymond Gay, 2025

A FINAL WORD ON LAW

Many Christians will assume that because I have placed Law/law in the non-faith category based on Galatians chapters 2 and 3, then I am automatically deriding it or against it in some way. CERTAINLY NOT!

In fact, St Paul states quite plainly in both Romans and Galatians that this is not the case. *Is the law then against the promises of God? Certainly not! For if there had been a law given which could have given life, truly righteousness would have been by the law. But the Scripture has confined all under sin,* (there's that preposition **under** again – comment mine) *that the promise by faith in Jesus Christ might be given to those who believe.* Galatians 3:21, 22.

The solution came with one major event – the **GREAT INTERVENTION** of **FAITH** – the entrance of the **CHRIST**.

Strangely enough, law still plays a role in our daily lives; perhaps not in the way we may think. There is one thing for certain: the world, the flesh and the devil are continually conspiring to bring us back under law (compulsion)! Sometimes those three forces are disguised within the institutionalised church.

A huge problem in the church for nearly two thousand years has been that many believers have been 'led' into being under law. The reasons for this are probably 'legion'. Yet for equally many reasons, many believers have never been told that they're **not supposed to stay there.** They are meant to be walking in God's Spirit; walking by faith; being led by His Spirit. My respectful petition to church leaders generally is to at least tell people WHY they are 'under law'; or is it that many church leaders don't know themselves. This last statement is not meant to undermine those who lead churches around the globe. It is meant to encourage leaders to enable their chargers to begin their journey to maturity in the Lord as soon as possible – to embody the teaching of Romans 8:14.

Legalism

Essentially legalism is taking any of the three or more types of law, as discussed above, and **turning it into a compulsive feature of our lives**.

We can utilise Judaic (or any other religious-based) law as a compulsive feature in our lives.

We can utilise national, state or provincial law as a compulsive feature in our lives (notwithstanding the 'rule of law').

We can utilise our own mentally -, or emotionally, - constructed law as a compulsive feature in our lives.

Sometimes these aspects of legalism can overlap.

Complementing the above, according to Dr R C Sproul in an excerpt from *How Can I Develop a Christian Conscience?* (Ligonier, 2016) [19], there are three aspects to so-called 'Christian' legalism; notably:

- *"...where one is concerned merely with the keeping of God's law as an end in itself."*
- *"The second form of legalism divorces the letter of the law from the spirit of the law. It obeys the letter but violates the spirit."*
- *"The third type of legalism adds our own rules to God's law and treats them as divine. It is the most common and deadly form of legalism."*

The points made by the renowned American theologian, Dr Sproul, who passed on to better things in 2017, quite adequately describes the essence of legalism.

Dr Sproul's first point is that legalism seeks to obey God's Law for its own sake without regard to the Covenant or Agreement that God established that eventually led to the Great Intervention. Our New Testament barrister, Paul, was adamant that Christians were not to rely on law if they were to grow in their faith, and that entailed not submitting ourselves to law as the goal. The late Dr Tim Keller goes even further than this by explaining that we can also be caught up in legalism to gain something from God or even rejecting God in some way. In *The Prodigal God* (Keller, 2008)[20], he asserts that *"Careful obedience to God's law may serve as a strategy for rebelling against God."* (ibid., p 37)

Second, and most significantly, is the adherence to the **letter of the law**. If you're remotely interested in the original Greek rendering, you'll no doubt have come across the word *logos*, which coincidentally is translated as 'word' in English. Although *logos* is the word used to describe Christ (the Word) in John chapter one, in other contexts it is used to denote language itself, as in the words I am typing now. We have the Bible as written words on papyrus, paper or on your digital screen. This is the 'letter' and can relate to the 'letter of the law'. But when the *logos* comes alive in us in the form of Christ and His Holy Spirit, then we have the 'spirit of the law' or to be consistent with Paul's teachings, the fulfilling of the law through the Spirit.

DESIRING TO BE UNDER LAW

You may also have noticed in the Galatian letter to whom Paul was directing his invective. He was addressing those who **desired to be under the law**! We have those people even today. In fact, I would venture to say that some Christians, many of whom would say that they are free, **prefer obeying laws to walking in the Spirit (or even a convoluted mixture of both!).** **WHY** do they do this? And **WHY** do some of this world's church leadership want to keep them there?

Part of the answer can be found in the photo below. Many of you may have seen this fascinating artwork by the famous American artist, Zenos Frudakis, found in Philadelphia, Penn., USA. It is titled *Freedom Sculpture*[21] and it was constructed in 2001. The photo below depicts only part of this sculpture.

There is much that can be gleaned from this depiction of a figure gradually breaking free from whatever is holding it back, but for this particular **L** plate, let's just focus in on the figure on the extreme left. It is obviously bound by its constraints:

it is completely *immobile*;

it is completely *restrained;*

it is unable to *express itself* except maybe by limited speech*;*

it is unable to *make its own decisions;* and most importantly

it is *completely under another's control;*

nobody is able to help this figure.

Many of us are exactly like this figure. We are *immobile*; we are *restrained*; we are unable to *express ourselves* in the way Christ had originally intended.

And yet some may say: *"Oh how safe and secure we feel!"; "Isn't it great to know exactly what we need to do!"; "Isn't it wonderful to know that in this position we'll never have to make another decision or mistake again!"*

The left-hand side of this sculpture illustrates the essence of **LEGALISM**.

But what screams out to me most of all when I see this photo is that many of us do **not want to be helped out of this!** Many of us would prefer to **be UNDER LAW!** Many of us *'desire to be under the law'* (Gal. 4:21), which may be one of the reasons why Paul referred to the Galatian Christians as **'foolish'**.

Although we are restrained, we would rather not have to **make our own decisions in Christ**, or to put it another way, **take on the responsibility of being led by the Holy Spirit**. And with great empathy for my early Galatian brothers and sisters in Christ, **this is indeed the scariest challenge of all!**

It is easier to obey a set of laws, rules, regulations, statutes, boundaries or whatever – something that is **compulsory** and does not incorporate the free will that God gave us as part of His initial creation.

And why would some members of the universal church's leadership want people to remain like this? The reasons over the last two thousand years have been legion; maybe because it is easier to control their congregations to save themselves a lot of heartache, or is there another less obvious reason that I shall explore when we reach the last two **L** plates?

LEGALISM AS A MENTALITY OR MINDSET

One of the most disturbing and deceitful aspects of legalism is that it can and does so easily become a constant way of thinking. We are just not able to help ourselves in this regard.

LEGALISM is as much a MINDSET as it is an unhealthy, unhelpful obsession with LAW.

We take scriptures that are no longer meant for guiding New Testament believers and we rigidly adhere to them at the cost of our liberty; our ability to take our own responsibility for being led by the Holy Spirit.

We make up our own rules about life and stick to them with a sense of compulsion that indeed leads to compulsiveness; possibly leading to a mental health issue later on.

We even take New Testament scriptures and turn them into rules etched in stone. No doubt you can think of a few right now.

"*...the most common and deadly form of legalism*" was how Dr Sproul summed up this type of mindset in his third point above.

This is not a healthy way of thinking about our walk with God. Some of we Christians are so caught up in the 'letter of the law', that we forget that law is a background to where the real action is. Sure it's still there, but

LEGALISM AS A MENTALITY OR MINDSET

we do not have law at the forefront of our thinking lives. It exists only to show us where we have derailed ourselves or been derailed so that we can be placed back on the path as quickly as possible. And that path is simply being led by His Holy Spirit.

My relationship with God is not based on law; or a legalistic mindset as a guide.

REVERENCE VERSUS RELIGION / RITUAL

In mentioning those "who desire to be under the law", or more forcefully stated in the Con Lit NT version "who **want** to be under law", it is vital that we understand the difference between a healthy and whole reverence for God and one based merely upon religious observance and/or ritual. Some people base their lives on rituals, as it seems to give them anchor points along the way. Without them they can't live. It becomes unhealthy compulsive behaviour. This may be fine for a while, but that lifestyle will eventually unravel and prove baseless.

Is a 'rite of passage' though a wrong thing to have? Not necessarily. A rite of passage is usually a one-off occasion; a milestone in someone's life that is recognised by one's community and celebrated as such. You've taken a step forward. The same could be said of the traditions that accompany a wedding ceremony or an academic graduation. The rituals to which I refer are usually habitual self-made laws that we impose upon ourselves to acquire a form of redemption or peace within ourselves.

A true reverence for God is borne out of relationship with Him; the maturing process that is spoken of in Romans 8 verse 14. Only as we walk in the Holy Spirit can we even begin to understand, appreciate and partake of His Holiness and Gravity. The older I grow as a Christian person, the more I am realising this truth. I am naturally lost in my foolishness and irreverence; however, as I surrender to His leading the miracle begins to take place. That sense of awe and reverence begins to fill my empty life.

LEGALISM AS EVANGELISM

There is only one set of circumstances in which the apostle Paul allows Christians to be "under law". In 1 Corinthians 9: 19-23, he places himself in servanthood mode for the sole purpose of winning a large range of people to Christ, despite experiencing the liberty to which he was called (Rf. Gal. 5:13, 14 to be discussed more fully later).

"For, being free of all, I enslave myself to all, that I should be gaining the more. And I became to the Jews as a Jew, that I should be gaining Jews; to those under law as under law (not being myself under law), that I should be gaining those under law; to those without law as without law (not being without God's law, but legally Christ's), that I should be gaining those without law. I became as weak to the weak, that I should be gaining the weak. To all I have become all, that I should undoubtedly be saving some. Now all am I doing because of the evangel, that I may be becoming a joint participant of it." (Con Lit NT)

The original King James version gave us the well-used saying, *"I have become all things to all men"* as in verse 22. This verse alone demonstrates the heart of Paul; that he was prepared to sacrifice his own liberty for the sake of others, that they may be won for Jesus. (A pastor I once knew in South Carolina testified that he preached in a southern church whose members did not believe in the display of jewellery of any type. He wondered why his message was bouncing back at him. The Lord advised him to take off his wedding ring and for his wife to discard her earrings. On the second occasion he preached, those folk responded and rejoiced in his message. We're unsure as to whether the absent ring or earrings was the key factor; but that's a pretty big coincidence.)

Yet, and this is the big YET, St Paul berates the Galatian regional churches for throwing away their liberty in their own progress towards godly maturity!

It is one thing to place yourself 'under law' for the sake of leading those 'under law' to liberty in Christ; it is another thing entirely to **remain** 'under law' yourself in the privacy of your own mindset because you believe that that is the end game of your Christian walk.

Let us reiterate the teaching of Jesus through Paul; that the main purpose of law in the grace dispensation is to bring people out from 'under law' or 'without law', or even without strength, into the amazing strength that being led by the Holy Spirit can bring. This is the end game for Christians during their lives here on planet Earth.

NO LEGALISM IN RELATIONSHIP

In devotionals I have often referred to my family and the close relationships we share. Each of our children are mature adults with amazing children of their own. When referring to offspring, Romans chapter 8 and verse 14 uses the expression "sons of God", nowadays perceived as a generic term. It is interesting to note the various words used in *koine* (the Greek of the 'man-in-the-street', the language mainly used in the New Testament) for our word "children" or "sons". The following list (transliterated into English) will indicate the significance of the above verse in Romans:

- *brephos*: interestingly a term used for both new born or unborn children (this could be helpful for some folks reading this book) and infant or toddler;
- *nepios*: a babe without the full power of speech;
- *paidion*: a little or young lad or child below the age of puberty;
- *pais*: a lad, boy or servant;
- *teknon*: one born, a child or youth;
- *huios*: a son, descendant, offspring – implying maturity.

In the same way that I might be called a child of my late parents, even though I'm rapidly approaching my three score years and ten, the implications of the words 'teknon' and 'huios' could be misconstrued. One academic source implies that teknon is a child of either sex and that huios indicates a male child only. If this is correct, does this mean that only male children get to be led by the Holy Spirit according to Romans 8:14? "Certainly not!", as Paul again would have said.

The use of the word 'huios' in this verse is significant because it heavily implies 'a mature, grown-up child who has been positioned' (Gooding, 1962) [22]. A person who has learned through many mistakes, sufferings and even through sins of commission and omission, to be brought back to be led by the Holy Spirit can surely claim some level of maturity. There are times when, like Paul, I still feel like the chief of sinners (1 Timothy 1:15), yet God has led me a certain distance along the path of maturity. This path is taking me away from my foolish Galatian tendencies, one of legalism and/or lawlessness. As one is "being led by God's spirit (sic), these are sons (mature sons or daughters – my interpretation only) of God." I have been taught through many bitter lessons to both be and act maturely as a father to his own children.

Do we want to be mature Christians?
Then let's learn how to be led by His Spirit.

So in referring to my children as mentioned above, my visits to them have taken on a changed characteristic. Knowing that my sons, daughters and their spouses have their own level of maturity, I am very careful not to barge in to their households with my own overbearing or egotistical agenda. I don't start shouting out orders and demands as I was inclined to do when they themselves were *paidion*. They have their own *paidion* now for whom to be responsible.

It is my responsibilty and privilege to generate and maintain relationship; not to be bogged down by familial legalism (or lawlessness as the case may be). When God fellowshipped with Adam and Eve in the Garden of Eden, there was no legalism or lawlessness, but relationship and maturity, admittedly from God anyway. This is the way in which I want to relate to my family; not ruling the roost as a misguided 'head of the home' or old testament-like patriarch. I now want to be led by the Holy Spirit, with His accompanying fruit (Rf. Gal 5:22,23), not in the foolish ways in which I tried to be a father and a husband years ago.

Our prayer for our children is that they and their descendants become not so much law-abiding citizens (as much as that is the loving thing to be for the sake of our society), but Christ-abiding citizens according to John chapter 15 and verses 1 to 8.

The quicker we can move from our foolishness into being led by the Holy Spirit, the quicker we can progress into a mature way of life with God and others; a life of completion.

[CONCERNING CHILDREN

There is a 'doctrine' these days, and believed by some in Christian schooling, that all children enrolled are automatically children of God. That may be so in a general creation sense, as we are all created in God's image, and is especially important to staff and parents in the way each child is treated.

Yet it is not scripturally correct in the issue of salvation. Unless anyone is born again, they cannot begin to be led by the Holy Spirit consistently and meaningfully in the way Paul tried to persuade his Galatian brothers and sisters. They can be drawn by the Holy Spirit to receive salvation, and THEN the journey begins in that sense. Eventually they must be able to make their own decisions concerning their faith. This is why the apostle Paul, specifically addressing children in his letters, tells them to *"...be obeying your parents, in the Lord, for this is just. 'Honor your father and mother' (which is the first precept with a promise), that it may be becoming well with you, and you should be a long time on the earth."* (Ephesians 6:1-3 Con Lit NT). Note here that Paul refers back to the law, quoting the fifth commandment in Exodus 20 and verse 12. It is assumed that children, like anyone else who have not received Christ, are automatically 'under law' as they have not begun to walk in the Holy Spirit, as implied in Galatians 5:18. There are, of course, those children that have begun their journey with God and are learning to be led by the Holy Spirit. Are they excused from wearing their school uniforms if required to do so? 'Certainly not!' Paul again might say. They are the ones who WANT to wear them, and wear them well. Why? As Paul again addresses children: *"...obey your parents in all things, for this is well pleasing in the Lord."* (Colossians 3 verse 20, Con Lit NT). The motivation to **want to please God** (and to do the right thing by others) grows exponentially with the maturing process of being led by His Holy Spirit.

Roadblock lifted – back on the main road.]

THE PREACHERS WHO KNEW ENOUGH!

Allow me to finish these observations with a story and a quote. When I was a young man in the Lord, I attended a New Year's conference with a few friends and fellow disciples of mine at Stanwell Tops in New South Wales. This was 1976 and the main speaker was Argentinian Pastor Juan Carlos Ortiz of *"we don't argue, we just hug you!"* fame. Before an afternoon session, my friends and I were kicking around a football as young blokes do, when an American guy approached us and asked to join in. We magnanimously agreed and included him in our riotous activity. When it was time to enter the auditorium we told our new friend that we might catch up later with our footy. We appreciated him joining us and thought what a likeable bloke he was. Upon entering the session, the hundreds of delegates were led in worshipping God and then the afternoon speaker was introduced. Lo and behold it was our new football buddy from the States – Pastor Jerry Cook! What a brother in Christ! This illustrated a WWJD example for me at the time, although Ps. Cook would have used the acronym WWJB: **WHO WOULD JESUS BE?** Yes, Jesus Himself would have joined in our game and had a great time with us before ministering to us. Jerry had shown us the significance of relationship and not burdensome legalism.

Which segues nicely back to a quote from his widow, Pastor Barbara Cook, who preached at the Southside Christian Renewal Centre in southern

Brisbane (now Life Church) twenty years later in 1996 and the day after my fortieth birthday. I wrote her quote down in the back of my Bible and it has been etched in my heart and mind ever since. She preached that ***"with legalism, you never know that what you have done is enough!"*** [23]

I type these lines with tearful eyes, knowing how much the late Pastor Jerry Cook and his widow blessed yours truly on two separate occasions; by demonstrating that walking in Jesus' Spirit will always be enough!

LEGALISM	Gal. 5:1, 13, 18; Matt. 23:24 Luke 15: 11 - 32	"under the law": a strict adherence to the letter of the law; is most often a mentality – a "yoke of bondage" – your own law! "straining at gnats"; Elder son's flesh.

© Geoffrey Raymond Gay, 2025

LICENCE

Most of us have a licence to drive a vehicle and/or to ride a motorcycle. A few students that we have taught over the years have earned a licence to fly an airplane. Most students back in the day used to look forward to receiving a pen licence in primary or elementary school. In many countries, a licence is required to get married. And then, of course, the fictional James Bond has a licence to kill (notwithstanding the sixth commandment)!

So, what then is a licence and how is that relevant to the **LICENCE** which is referred to in the context of this book?

**A LICENCE gives or grants you permission to
do something or not do something.**

Whether it's permission to drive a car, ride a motorbike, fly a plane, push a pen in primary school, get hitched or legally do nasty things for the British Secret Service, a person needs to be given or granted permission for those activities, usually by someone officially or legally appointed to do so through legislation of some type. Even a police service cannot do anything beyond what legislation permits them to do or not do. Ironically, in most of these examples, **you need a law to say that you can have a licence.**

A work colleague of mine once pointed out to our teaching staff during a devotional time that we can all give ourselves a licence (or permission) to be led by the Holy Spirit - and he was absolutely correct!

Also recently, a beautiful little book by debut author Catherine 'Kitty' Green, entitled *Licence to Love: Driven by Faith* (Green, 2024) [24], provides visual confirmation of the above-mentioned licence on Christ-centered car registration plates in the USA.

Notwithstanding these little gems, and for the purpose of this disquisition only, the word licence will be used to mean **permission that we grant ourselves to do our own thing, independently from God.** This fits in with the traditional use of the word **licentiousness** which is occasionally used in some older Biblical versions; albeit with strong sexual connotations (ref. Mark 7:22; Romans 13:13; Ephesians 4:19 and 1 Peter 4:3. and Gal. 5:19 in the NKJV).

In his book, *The Problem of Doing Your Own Thing* (Mumford, 1973) [25], significantly published in the early 1970s when the so-called 'charismatic movement' was in full flow contemporaneous with the 'Jesus Revolution', the Rev Bob Mumford drove home a message few of us at the time wanted to hear.

He asked: *"Is it possible to know and understand the things of the Spirit, grab them to ourselves and go our own ways? The answer is a resounding YES!"*. (ibid., p15) He went on to say: *"One important principle which we need to realize is this: the ultimate law in all the Universe is the will of God. There is no law above the will of God"*. (ibid.)

He follows this later with: *"When God's will crosses our will – that is when we discover the spirit within us that responds, 'But I want to do my own thing!' We super-impose our own will on God's will ... and this is lawlessness."* (ibid., p17) Rev Mumford explained that we inherited this *"from our father Adam"* (ibid.) and that it refers not to acts of sin necessarily but *"with the inward nature of obedience"*. (ibid., p16)

This is a very hard pill for us Christians to swallow. Yet there is hope for us with this final quote from Rev. Mumford: *"Each one of us will have to discover for himself his own spirit of lawlessness. Because we have thrown off outward sin, we have difficulty recognizing that the spirit of rebellion, the spirit of anarchy, is at work in our lives. What God is really after is to write* His *law on our hearts."*. (ibid., p18)

[CONCERNING ANARCHY

Many of you will be familiar with a popular modern symbol, even used in the fashion industry, of a circle enclosing a capital letter A. This symbol stands for anarchy and is considered by most Christians as being a symbol of rebellion at best, or Satanic at worst. Granted it does have occultic overtones nowadays; hence it would be beneficial to understand its underlying philosophy.

Also, we tend to confuse the term 'revolution' with the term anarchy; so we also call the bomb-throwing revolutionaries 'anarchists'. The terms can be linked; albeit there is a fundamental difference concerning the nature of an anarchist.

In 2005 I came across a group of 'experienced' anarchists who had set up a stand at the annual commemorations of the anniversary of the Eureka Stockade rebellion in Ballarat, wherein miners had declared the Republic of Victoria in protest against the mining policies of Queen Victoria's colonial Governor in 1854. Although the original miners were revolutionaries, these modern-day supporters saw themselves differently. These peaceful demonstrators were merely emphasising that they did not want law of any type in their lives. They simply wanted to live their lives without government interference in any form, as they believed they were 'good' citizens despite what people thought of them. They weren't throwing Molotov cocktails, shouting offensive slogans or spitting at police like revolutionaries are reputed to do. They did not want to overthrow the government and/or place themselves in positions of power like the original Eureka rebels were doing. They were genteel people to talk to with a Ghandi-style agenda of peaceful 'resistance'.

The thing we miss about the 'true' anarchist is that they sincerely believe they are inherently 'good' people; thereby living 'good' lives and not hurting anyone. Thus it is a question of the 'nature of man', to use a generic term. This is also described more fully in Baron Lloyd of Hampstead's book: *The Idea of Law* (Lloyd, 1973, pp 18 – 25) [26]. The difference or distinctive for Christians is that Paul categorically stated in Romans that "all have sinned and fallen short of the glory of God" (Rom. 3:23). Christians believe that we are inherently NOT 'good', stemming from the Fall, thus eventually necessitating law, from which faith in the form of Jesus Christ had to rescue or save us. Saying we are not 'good' may be a simplistic way of saying that our nature had fallen.

LICENCE

The revolutionaries do not care about whether they are bad or not; they just want to take over government and make the decisions themselves for their jurisdiction. Politics after all is who gets to make the decisions; followed by what decisions are actually made. The 'true' anarchist doesn't want a jurisdiction in the first place, but the irony is, because they are 'good' people and do not want to hurt others, this may never happen; unless, of course, they are all shipwrecked alone on a lush tropical island. Enter stage left the *Lord of the Flies* (Golding, 1954) [27] universe and check out how that finished up; given that the title is translated Beelzebub as in Matthew chapter 12 and verse 24! In William Golding's narrative, governance on the island for the schoolboys began as a parliamentary democracy (remember the conch shell for each speaker?). A benevolent monarchy would have also sufficed. Eventually a group of the boys broke away and formed their own type of anarchy – yahoos as mentioned above; albeit under the shadow of one boy. What began as so called anarchy quickly turned into dictatorship under that one boy, Jack. Political vacuums do not last long. The revolutionary dictators will soon take over!).

We Christians on the other hand believe that we need rescuing from our inherited 'badness' or sin, leading to the guard and the tutor, then to the coming of faith and release! We are free in the loving arms of godly government whose members understand the purpose of law in our lives.

Interestingly, and for fans of the *Blade Runner* movies, there exists a fictional concept called 'the Galatians Syndrome'. To quote a blogger named 'applesdontpee' on *reddit.com* [28], *"The replicant rebellion is to create a world where they can determine their own fate. They don't need man's laws to control them."* Furthermore, *"In a way, it's like the replicants are the gentiles and OG humans are the Hebrews. ...the girl supposedly died of a genetic disorder, so this 'Galatians Syndrome' – which symbolizes the fight to determine your own fate – was inherent in her; an inalienable right."* This is an intriguing piece of cyberpunk, combining the concepts of revolution and anarchy. Yet more intriguing is the reference to the star of this thesis - Paul's letter to the Galatians and its implied theme of who governs whom!

Detour finished – back on track)

THE VENN DIAGRAM FOR SOUL-SWINGERS

The insidious part of 'lawlessness', also translated as 'iniquity' in some versions of the scriptures, is that it not only covers our definition of licence in this study, but also crosses over to legalism *a la* a Venn diagram. Legalism is a form of licence in that even though we think we are doing God's will from a legal point of view (the letter of the law), it denies God His rightful place as our sovereign Lord in the everyday ebb and flow of our daily lives. Where is the spontaneous flow of the Spirit in our hearts that we can respond to with God as our Father, Jesus as His Son and Holy Spirit as our Comforter and constant Companion – a relational Trinity?

This is why the apostle Paul was so concerned. He even labelled what the Galatian assemblies were drifting into a "different (or distorted) evangel", with the admonition that those who preached such would be "anathema" or accursed; this being repeated for emphasis. (Gal. 1: 7-9 Con Lit NT)

What the apostle Paul was hoping and praying that the Galatian Christians would do is to "write His law on their hearts". What is God's will that we need to align our will with? **That of being led by Holy Spirit.** If we are taught to be led by the Holy Spirit, our licentiousness, both inwardly and outwardly, will begin to be assigned to the trash heap.

"Now I am saying, Walk in spirit, and you should under no circumstances be consummating the lust of the flesh. For the flesh is lusting against the spirit,

yet the spirit against the flesh. Now these are opposing one another, lest you should be doing whatever you may want." Gal. 5: 16, 17 (Con Lit NT)

How do we cease to do "whatever we may want"? How do we eliminate this tendency to personal licence, be it licentiousness, legalism or a spirit of rebellion? We need to learn how to "walk in His spirit".

| LICENCE | Gal. 5:13, Gal. 5:19 – 21; Matt. 23: 24; Luke 15: 11 - 32 | "above the law": giving ourselves permission to do whatever we want to do; "swallowing camels"; younger son's flesh. |

© Geoffrey Raymond Gay, 2025

LEGALISM, LICENCE AND SOUL-SWINGING !

One of the most significant verses that guided my thinking for this conversation is found in Matthew 23:24, when Jesus exclaims: *"Blind guides! straining out a gnat, yet swallowing a camel!"* (Con Lit NT) Notwithstanding the exegetical context of this exclamation in relation to temples, altars, tithes of mint, anise and cummin, justice mercy and faith, I find that there is a creation principle here that can't be ignored.

These words totally illustrate the difference between legalism and licence as discussed above. To be legalistic is to strain at every gnat; being finicky over the smallest little thing; getting anxious over the smallest element of doctrine; becoming obsessed over how many angels can fit on the point of a pin or what colour eyes the Virgin Mary had (as we used to argue over dinner!). Yes, with legalism there is straining, as Jesus indicated metaphorically. What a terrible way to live; yet some of our clinics treat folks who have suffered from this mindset. This is that poor figure constrained in Frudakis' sculpture. They are totally bound up, albeit being seemingly comfortable with that.

At the other end of the same pendulum is the reality of licence in each of our lives. When we choose to do what we want to do, we tend to 'swallow camels' as Jesus said. We allow ourselves to think, say and do very big things that saddens the very heart of God, as well as our loved ones. This list as we have seen is inexhaustible.

We 'sweat the small stuff' and let the big problems through.

There are three significant points to be made here from this confrontation with Christ:

First, notice that both the straining of gnats and the swallowing of camels are not different concepts to be dealt with separately. They are happening on the same 'spectrum', hence my use of the term 'pendulum' in the chart entitled: **The Aspirant Believer**. I once illustrated this in a staff devotional by attaching an object to a piece of string and swinging it from side to side shouting out "legalism!", "licence!", "legalism!", "licence!" at the end of each arc. A 'sound' teaching strategy, but after a while it was thoroughly annoying to everyone (indicative of much of my teaching career, no doubt!). Then again, the fact that Jesus had to point this out to his audience was probably annoying to Him as well.

Second, the spectrum or pendulum upon which these concepts : straining gnats – legalism; swallowing camels – licence; reside, is actually the Tree of the Knowledge of Good and Evil. Remember that tree? If we happen to believe in the theological 'principle of first mention' it takes on a much stronger significance once we receive a revelation of what this verse could be telling us.

In traditional Christian doctrine, this tree was supposed to have allowed the first humans to know what God already knew – the difference between good and evil. The serpent deceived the couple into believing that they would be getting in on the big secret; the knowledge that God was supposedly keeping from them. After all, God is nasty that way, isn't He; keeping blessings from His creation and allowing them to suffer? *"Certainly not!"* It may well be that there is certain knowledge that is not meant for us at this time. God is a big God after all and there is only a certain amount of knowledge that we can deal with in this dispensation (Moyo, 2025). [29]

In other words, the serpent created a fake problem and offered a fake solution – eat the fruit and you too can know what God knows; taking away any advantage that God thinks He has over you! The problem here is that our autonomous notion of good and evil is opposed to what God knows is good for us or evil for us.

This was the beginning of the notion of equity at a spiritual level and it was the first anthropogenic (human-generated) power play. If Adam and Eve had have eaten of the fruit, then gone on to eat from the Tree of Life, then they would have been doomed to eternal dying and pain, as the Tree of the Knowledge of Good and Evil automatically implied every human thought, word and deed. Adam and Eve were quite joyfully being led by God Himself in the paradise He had created for them. His deep desires for their success as humans was engraved on their hearts, as they were made in His image; although through free will, they had not yet allowed their walk with Him to mature them as His children (Rom 8:14). On the other hand, the 'accuser of the brethren' did not want God's creation to walk in His ways, so he got them focused on themselves rather than God. Satan wants us to revel in the subtleties of good and evil and to 'strain the gnats' and 'swallow the camels'. The devil wants us to keep perishing in our own ignorance – to be eternally frustrated and angry. After a while though we do get tired of eating from 'the tree of the knowledge of me and me'! Although His Holy Spirit is in us continually, we choose daily from which tree we want to eat.

Therefore, as the Tree of the Knowledge of Good and Evil exemplifies EVERY human-generated experience that we can name, we usually spend most of our lives swinging somewhere between each of the concepts mentioned above. We are **soul- swingers**, and at times we even allow ourselves, or are forced, to swing to the very extremities of each arc; implying that some of us only have small swings. Each anthropogenic experience takes on its own value; that of good or evil or somewhere in between these two. The terms 'good' and 'evil' become relative on this tree as we tend to mix up these definitions according to our predispositions or self-made habits. Fortunately, God sees it differently. We continually live in the Tree of the Knowledge of Good and Evil, thinking that we are living from the Tree of Life. Unlike Tarzan, we are swinging from branch to branch in the same tree – not getting anywhere! I suspect we are more like George of the Jungle, suffering intently from the battering we impose on ourselves! This was partly the problem the foolish Galatians had, and the problem from which they had to be delivered.

Third, Jesus had a specific audience for this astute observation about us humans – the Pharisees, whom He interestingly called "serpents" in Matthew 23:33! Throughout the gospel accounts in particular, this group of hardened religious legalists was the target of Christ's verbal arrows. And the point of this arrow was that Jesus was talking about the strained gnats and the swallowed camels **to the same group of people!** It wasn't that one type of person was straining at the gnats and another set of people over there were swallowing the camels. The Pharisees were doing both and probably at the same time, as it is possible to be a religious legalist AND do whatever we ourselves want to do independently of God. Remember Ps Keller's quote implying that legalism can be a form of rebellion? Such is the nature of the Tree of the Knowledge of Good and Evil.

Yes, folks, we do this most of the time, unless of course we are walking in His Spirit! We are soul-swingers and it accounts for much of what we do and what motivates us in our actions.

[CONCERNING THE STUDY OF THE 'MIND'

To many of our learned colleagues in the psychology / psychiatric field, this revelation may not gel with modern interpretations of motivations and actions. I can only interpret the scriptures as God gives me the ability, so I would be very interested to hear how my personal interpretations 'pass the pub test' (as we Aussies say) in clinics and universities. It is my intention to *"rightly divide the word of truth."* (2 Timothy chapter 2 and verse 15b)

Detour finished – back on track.)

SAMPLE SOUL-SWINGING

So, are there everyday examples of this revelation in our modern societies today? There is probably a legion of them, but I'll just stick to a couple to which you may relate.

I'm going to talk about a person whom I shall name Fred. Fred was the most atrocious driver in the whole of the state! Fred had great difficulty parking cars, passing cars, looking out for other drivers and generally displaying gross incompetence in driving. These could be excused by a 'lack of skills' but what was most irksome was Fred's penchant for using a hand-held mobile phone whilst dodging traffic with a car full of passengers. Of course this was not only dangerous (pointed out later when we discuss 'driving in the spirit'), but it is against the relevant state's law. Fred had a license, but Fred was always in danger of losing it. On the other hand, Fred was the most religious, legalistic person known around the place. Adherence to observance of days, rituals, literal interpretations of metaphors Jesus used in the context of church traditions, gave Fred a legalistic reputation despite seemingly having a loving and caring heart. Despite spending hours of the day endeavouring to be led by the spirit, Fred also spent much time on the soul-swinging pendulum from legalism to licence and back again! I'm not condemning this type of person, because I do exactly the same sorts of things myself wittingly or not; I'm a descendant of Adam and Eve after all!

SAMPLE SOUL-SWINGING

What's that old saying: "*same person, different hat*"? Maybe you are this type of person; there are plenty of us foolish Galatians around!

Gangs we see on TV are also an example of soul-swingers. Anarchists have already been discussed, but for the sake of convenience allow me to refer to the *Sons of Anarchy* [30], a popular show that depicts the joys, trials and heartaches of people who are both victims and generators of life-threatening problems (just about depicts every drama ever scripted, right?). As mentioned, despite the fact that I don't believe that this type of soul-swinger is technically an anarchist, we'll take a quick look at the soul-swinging characteristics in this type of gang and its members.

Why people, especially men, join gangs, should be left up to experts in that field, so I'm going to leave that one alone; almost. Yet I can point out two main aspects of their lives, as observed generally and as told to me by one member of a 'friendly' group in this sub-culture.

First, a gang itself can be extremely legalistic. Not only is it very tough getting into the gang in the first place, it is tough staying there. Very strict rules and regulations apply. Very few women are allowed in gangs, with even stricter rules applying to them. The way gang members relate to each other structurally is highly regimented. The society in which gang members operate is hierarchical; solidified in a rigid structure. This structure can attract those looking for the 'comfort' of regimentation, especially ones who are experienced in that structure. These types of gangs could almost be likened to cults.

Second, the lifestyle of gangs can be lawless or licentious. Some gangs engage in criminal activity. As a gang, fuelled from the top of their respective hierarchies, they do what they want to do, at times thumbing their noses at the 'decency of society'. Within their definition of 'liberty', they feel free to give gifts to sick children at Christmas; stop a whole lane of traffic so their brothers can make a turn into a venue; punish a brother for grassing to the police or even killing an ex-member.

The pendulum swing within the Tree of the Knowledge of Good and Evil is very evident in these two examples. Without being condemnatory to anyone with this book, I believe I have described the concept of soul-swinging in practical terms that we can all relate to in one form or another. What would the pendulum swing look like for you?

THAT PRODIGAL SON!

By now you will have noticed that our discussion has moved from a separate study of legalism and licence or lawlessness to a merging of the two. It is difficult at times to see that both concepts are an aspect of the same problem. If there is any parable that illustrates this perfectly, it is the story of what is traditionally titled *The Prodigal Son*; found in Luke chapter 15. Take some time now to read Jesus's parable from verses 11 to 31.

The late Ps Tim Keller, in his amazing book *The Prodigal God*, beautifully and gently explains this dilemma as exemplified by the two brothers in the story. (I implore you all to beg, borrow or buy a copy for yourself, and wear out a few highlighters while you're at it!)

Ps Keller's preferred title for this parable is: *The Two Lost Sons* (Keller, 2008., pXIV); an informal title that perfectly illustrates the mindset of any foolish Galatian. Without stretching the story out too far, the younger brother who squandered his father's wealth acted in licence or lawlessness; the elder brother with a legalistic mindset. The sin of the younger brother is obvious, even to non-Christians, but the sin of the elder brother gets lost in our own sense of self-righteousness. Keller puts it this way:

'Everybody knows that the Christian gospel calls us away from the licentiousness of younger brotherness, but few realize that it also condemns moralistic elder brotherness.' (ibid., p 67) He points out that the *'...targets of the story*

are not "wayward sinners" but religious people...' (ibid., p10) and that the elder brother's mindset *'...only leads to a slavish, begrudging compliance to the letter of the law.'* (ibid., p59)

With apologies to our late mentor, I could go on quoting him all day. But as the *piece de resistance* that harmonises his teaching with the concepts covered in this book, one last quote from him on this subject is instructive: *'There are some traditional-looking elder brothers that, as a release valve, maintain a secret life of younger brother behaviour.'* (ibid., p33) In other words, the same person swinging through the spectrum of human experiences on the one pendulum!

Let's hand those fruitless 'licences' back to the ultimate authority.

OFF TO THE RACES!

My maternal grandfather, John Crook, loved to spin yarns. Whether it was Quartermaster Sergeant Crook storming the beaches of Gallipoli in 1915 and then personally telling Field Marshal Blamey that he was way off course, or driving a horse and cart full of vegies to market with his dad at 3 o'clock in the morning, every so often he'd throw a joke in to spice up the topic whilst holding court. They were always very dated as he was born in the mid-1880s and because my immediate ancestors included horse-racing folk, there would often be a 'story' from the track.

One such 'story' described punter Charlie's prowess at betting on a sure thing at Flemington in Melbourne one day. Charlie and his friend, Jack, cheered as the field bolted from the barrier, but Charlie's nag suddenly turned around and raced off in the opposite direction! "Hey Charlie!" shouted Jack, "you're bloomin' 'orse is going east, not west!" "No worries, Jack," replied Charlie, "I backed it both ways!"

Any horse-racing enthusiast will understand what an 'each way bet' is, with the expression 'hedging your bets' almost synonymous with this concept.

For the last two millenia, we Christians have been very good at having an 'each way bet' with our doctrines; backing our horse both ways. Admittedly some doctrines have been extremely difficult to understand, especially in the context of the laws we have made for ourselves to complicate the societies in which our Christian lives were meant to flourish.

One of those doctrines has of course concerned our walk with the Holy Spirit. What has that looked like over those two millenia and what is it supposed to look like now? In the grace dispensation (AD) what is God supposed to do and what are we supposed to do? Oftentimes in our church lives, there has been a paralysing Mexican standoff; mostly starring the misunderstanding of how laws are to be used or discarded.

We invariably end up with a mixture of laws we think we need to obey and a slight sense of the leading of the Spirit; ending up with a form of super-spiritual traditionalism.

A late pastor of mine, the Rev A S Worley (of the discarded jewellery church visit as above), was the principal of a South Carolina Bible school in Walhalla called Faith Training Center that I attended back in 1977. He once held up a glass jar filled with oil and water during one of our lectures (the oil in this illustration should not be confused with allusions to oil representing the Holy Spirit in certain scriptures). The water could not mix with the oil and vice versa. The purpose of the demonstration? Our Christian life is not a mixture of faith and law, grace and compulsion or the Tree of Life and the Tree of the Knowledge of Good and Evil. To use a well-known saying from the 'deep south': *"That dog don't hunt!"*

On numerous occasions during AD, the church universal has attempted to try this with confusing results. We've meditated upon laws and lawlessness, researched them, thumped the pulpit with them, made people feel guilty about them, churned them into a mixture of Old Covenant and New Covenant: anything from tattoos to tithing, tenets to the Ten Commandments **WITHOUT FIRST SUBMITTING THEM UNDER the AUTHORITY of ROMANS 8:14 and GALATIANS 5:18!**

OFF TO THE RACES!

Obviously, like oil and water, faith and gambling do not mix, but if you want your "bloomin' 'orse" to win the race, face it in the right direction. Let's stop having 'each way bets' about our doctrines and focus on what it means to walk in the Holy Spirit.

THE TEN COMMANDMENTS IN THE CLASSROOM

Recently there have been a number of states in the USA who have attempted to re-institute the Ten Commandments onto the walls of their public classrooms. In a digital article entitled: **Some US lawmakers want more Christianity in the classroom. Trump could embolden their plans** (Balingit, 2025) [31], AP education writer Moriah Balingit outlines a move by conservative Christians in the southern states particularly who wish to test *"the separation of church and state by inserting Bible references into reading lessons and requiring teachers to post the Ten Commandments."*. She continues with: *"The efforts come as President-elect Donald Trump prepares to take office pledging to champion the First Amendment right to pray and read the Bible in school, practices that are already allowed as long as they are not government-sponsored."*. The article concludes with: *"In Louisiana, Republicans passed a law requiring every public school classroom to post the Ten Commandments, which begin with "I am the Lord thy God. Thou shalt have no other gods before me." Families have sued."*

Of course, as a Christian, I have no objection to these inclusions in any school anywhere in the world, especially as I once had close contact with personnel from the Russian Ministry of Education who were doing similar things in the immediate post-Soviet era throughout their own country. Ironically on this field it seems like the Americans are having to play catch-up football with the Russians!

Yet there is one foreboding feature about these intentions that I find irritating and frustrating. By posting the Ten Commandments on their classroom walls, they are making a statement about the 'Judeo' part of our Judeo-Christian societal foundation. **But where is the Christian part?**

Were we to post the Ten Commandments on our classroom walls, which I'm used to seeing as a retired Christian schoolteacher anyway, I would want to see another poster placed next to it, above it, overshadowing it **that places the Ten Commandments in its proper Judeo-Christian context.**

Let me make a respectful suggestion, and yes, you guessed it; **let the extra poster reflect the New Testament teaching found in the PAULINE REVELATION: that being ROMANS 8:14 and GALATIANS 5:18 or any other set of verses that properly expresses the intent behind ACTUALLY FULFILLING the LAW.**

THE PENDULUM OF THE SOUL
(swinging through the vast spectrum of human experiences in thought, word and deed)

(The TREE of the KNOWLEDGE of GOOD and EVIL - Gen. 2:17)

LAW	Gal. 3:19, 23 - 26; 4:1-3 Rom. 7:12	our 'protector' and 'tutor' (guardian and steward) until faith (Christ) came!"
LEGALISM	Gal. 5:1, 13, 18; Matt. 23:24 Luke 15: 11 - 32	"under the law": a strict adherence to the letter of the law; is most often a mentality – a "yoke of bondage" – our own law! "straining at gnats"; elder son's flesh.
LICENCE **(Lawlessness)**	Gal. 5:13, Gal. 5:19 – 21; Matt. 23: 24 Luke 15: 11 - 32	above the law: giving ourselves permission to do whatever we want to do; "swallowing camels"; younger son's flesh.

© Geoffrey Raymond Gay, 2025

PART THREE

~

FOREGROUND

PART TWO

THUNDERBIRD

EMERGING FROM THE GALATIAN GLOOM

*Suleyman woke with a start when he heard the volume of the elder rise with an exclamation of the word **"freedom!"**. He had drifted off for a few moments and was keen to rejoin the discussion, albeit only for hearing and meditation. But how many people did he know of in this region and around the Roman empire itself that were yearning for this very thing: **freedom**. Could this Paul be planning to set slaves free, just like the infamous Spartacus (Brittanica, 2025) [32]? This would be an exciting change to the mundane existence in which he found himself.*

But now what was he hearing from the mouth of the elder whose demeanour was cheerier now that he had read beyond Paul's rebukes? There seemed to be certain things that these Jewish believers were not required to do any more – something to do with their laws. His attention was quickly captured by an utterance concerning, of all things, circumcision. What in Zeus' name are they talking about? How embarrassing! I wish they'd talk about something else.

So what now are we called to? Freedom? There's that treasonous word again. I hope the Roman guards aren't marching around in the market square hearing all of this. We'll all be in very big trouble!

Suddenly another word cropped up amongst a raft of so-called evil things being listed: drunkenness. His mood was lowered quickly as he thought of his own father who had been killed in a drunken brawl when Suleyman was only an infant. He wished he had known his father more, and wished even more that his father had been able to hear the gentle voice of the elder. Could there have been some sort of hope for his father?

He didn't have to wait long for hope for himself, for disturbing his brief reverie came some of the most beautiful words he had ever heard: love, joy, peace. And then something called patience which he could use a lot more of himself. Goodness and kindness came to his ears and he soaked up the thought of him never having to be bullied again. The rest of the audience were pausing after every word to discuss the impact of each so it gave him more time to meditate on each new idea.

Faithfulness. Wasn't that being full of faith? Well, that makes sense I suppose because you couldn't be a believer otherwise! Suleyman's young mind was spinning with possibilities. Meekness. Who couldn't be meek nowadays with that Roman scum on our doorsteps harassing us daily? I guess I'll have to stop being arrogant myself if I have to remember peace as well, he ruminated.

Self-control? No, surely not; although Suleyman had once heard from a local scout that to be a good soldier you had to control your feelings. Maybe that's not so bad after all.

Suleyman finally finished racing through his thoughts with a sense of comfort.

...to be continued.

Liberty

THE MISSION STATEMENT

About thirty years ago, I started working at the inter-systemic level of independent education in the Australian state of Queensland. Like many corporate groups, both for-profit and not-for-profit, we were always looking out for the best mission statements going around at that time. It was strange to me that corporations had mission statements, yet individuals were not expected to have one. We all know that go-getters are meant to have goals, but do we have a pithy, memorable statement that is foundational to our own lives; an anchor point that strengthens our resolve and serves as our life's reference point?

I decided to put this to our Lord and the reply was swift and decisive. It was a verse of scripture that had cropped up every so often in the early days of my Christian walk. Yes, a passage of scripture can be your personal mission statement!

<u>My Personal Mission Statement is:</u>
"Stand fast therefore in the liberty by which Christ has made us free, and do not be entangled again with a yoke of bondage."
(Gal. 5:1 NKJV)

The Concordant Literal NT expresses this in an interesting way:

"For freedom Christ frees us! Stand firm, then, and be not again enthralled with the yoke of slavery."

What is this elusive thing called liberty? Allow me to offer a personal definition:

**LIBERTY grants me the freedom and ability
to be who God desires me to be;
and to do the things God wants me to do.**

How many Aussie baby boomers out there recall a rock band about fifty years ago called The Masters Apprentices? I remember the chorus of the song It's Because I Love You (Ford and Keays 1971):

Oooooh, do what you wanna do, be what you wanna be, Yeaaaaah!

The sentiments underlying those lyrics accurately capture the foundational mindset that has dominated the last fifty years of western civilisation. Compare these thoughts with my definition of divine liberty above. Yes, as much as I liked The Masters Apprentices back in the day, their definition of freedom is the direct opposite of my personal one.

There is one thing for certain; we are NOT able to enjoy that freedom if we are all tangled up in sin; if we are enthralled with a yoke of slavery! This is the very reason why Christ (faith) came, as declared in Galatians chapter 3. He wants to set us free to eat abundantly of the fruit from the Tree of Life, not continually banging our heads swinging with gay abandon from branch to branch on the Tree of the Knowledge of Good and Evil!

Have I 'drifted' from this personal mission from time to time? Yes, indeed. This is a major part of my personal confession. Even our apostolic brother, Paul, had difficulty in these areas. Just read Romans chapter 7 for an outstanding explanation of the dilemma we face daily. His triumphal conclusion in Romans 8:2? *"For the law of the Spirit of life in Christ Jesus has made me free from the law of sin and death."* (NKJV)

STANDING FIRM

There is a distinct difference between **standing firm** and **soul-swinging**. With the former we have our feet firmly planted; we are immovable and steady in our convictions. With the other we are 'all over the shop' as the saying goes in the realm of our thoughts, motivations, actions, feelings and consequences.

'Immovable' doesn't sound like freedom; it rather looks like the sculpture depicting legalism, as above. But 'immovable' describes our **resolve**, as this is what is forged through the fires of suffering and provides us with the motivation that we need for both endurance and direction in the Holy Spirit.

If there is one prevailing theme in all of the apostle Paul's letters to the saints, our earlier brothers and sisters in Christ, it is to not allow anything to get in between us and our Lord Jesus. For that to happen, we need to stand firm!

OUR CALLING

To what then have we been called? How are we to spend the rest of our lives being and doing? What is it that challenges us from day to day that the penitent on the cross never had to face; albeit with no complaints from him! Our divine barrister answered this succinctly:

> *"For you, brethren, have been called to liberty; only do not use (sic) liberty as an opportunity for the flesh, but through love serve one another. For all the law is fulfilled in one word, even (sic) in this: 'You shall love your neighbor as yourself'."*
> (Gal. 5: 13, 14 NKJV)

Again, the Concordant Literal NT rendering is just as impactful:

> *"For you were called for freedom, brethren, only use (sic) not the freedom for an incentive to the flesh, but through love be slaving for one another. For the entire law is fulfilled in one word, in this(sic): "You shall love your associate as yourself.' "* (Cf. 1 Peter 2: 15, 16 NKJV)

LIBERTY AND LOVE FULFIL THE LAW

Please advise me if I have read this incorrectly, but it seems to me that the word **LIBERTY** is heavily associated with the word **LOVE**; and in placing those words together in association with each other, we end up with the fulfilling of the concept called **LAW**. As we have observed above:

LEGALISM is being **UNDER the LAW;**

LICENCE (lawlessness) is being **"ABOVE the LAW"** (not a biblical term, but one used commonly in our society); yet

LIBERTY is LOVE that **FULFILS the LAW!**

They fulfil the **SPIRIT of the LAW**, not the **LETTER of the LAW**.

We now have a **HEART of FLESH** (not to be confused with the 'works of the flesh' in Gal. 5:19) and not of **STONE**, as in Ezekiel 36:26.

I am **NOT**:

under law;

under a law;

under the law;

under my own law; or

under your law.

My **MOTIVATION** now is to **FULFIL LAW** through **LIBERTY** which enables me to **LOVE**.

PART FOUR

~

TAKING GROUND

AND THE GALATIANS REJOICE!

Suleyman had finished his bread and sipped the last of his water as it appeared that the elder was beginning to bring Paul's letter to a conclusion. He talked about a spirit of meekness – there was that word again – and something about bearing each other's burdens. This being an action of love was supposed to fulfil the law, whatever that meant, but he was quickly becoming attuned to the language and tone of the apostle's letter and starting to warm to its message.

By now the rest of the assembly was starting to stir from their lethargy and raising their voices with shouts of encouragement to their elder and to Paul in absentia. The elder's lips were no longer drawn downwards but now sported a triumphant grin and he began to twirl around and sing with the rest of the believers as if they were celebrating someone's wedding and had forgotten all about Suleyman tucked away snuggly against the back wall.

Amid the shouting and clapping, Suleyman tried to remember some of the last lines of Paul's letter. **"For in Christ Jesus neither circumcision nor uncircumcision is anything, but a new creation. And whoever shall observe the elements by this rule, peace be on them, and mercy, also on the Israel of God."**

Peace, thought Suleyman. Can this Christ Jesus really make me brand new and give me peace? With a warmth in his chest he couldn't explain, he closed his eyes in contentment and slowly succumbed to his daydreaming. He suddenly found himself in the most beautiful field he had ever seen, and was wrapped up in the arms of Jesus Himself, twirling around with joy just as he had seen the believers do. He knew that something had changed inside him as he could not take his eyes off the One who had purchased his freedom.

He woke from his slumber to find the elder and some other believers leaning over him. He looked up into the elder's eyes, and, with a slight touch of embarrassment, muttered, "I believe I just met Yehoshua your Messiah." The elder smiled down at him and placed his hand upon his head.

"My son, thank you so much for delivering this very important message from our brother. What is your name?"

"Suleyman," replied the youth.

"Ahh, meaning He who is a Man of Peace, I surmise. We rejoice with you, young brother, for you have now met your Messiah as well, your Prince of Peace and His love for you will know no end!"

LOVE

The PLUMB LINE of the SPIRIT (steadfast vertical orientation)		
(The TREE of LIFE) Gen. 3: 22 -23		
LIBERTY / LED by the SPIRIT	Gal. 5:1,13-14, Gal. 5:18; 2 Cor. 3: 17; Rom. 8:14	**"NOT UNDER LAW"**: learning the spirit of the law; practising the presence of the spirit; mature 'sonship'.
LOVE	Gal. 5:13-14 Gal. 6: 2	**"fulfils the law"**: serving one another in love.

© Geoffrey Raymond Gay, 2025

And so we come to **LOVE** and its intimate connection with our walk in the Holy Spirit. Many will say that since we gave our lives to Christ, or said "yes to Jesus", we are automatically walking in His Spirit and are unable to walk otherwise. The Bible doesn't necessarily agree with that position. In my understanding, there are two main reasons why.

First, the Bible clearly indicates that we can stray from His leading and go back to independent living; either legalistically or licentiously or both. Being led by His Spirit is a daily choice even though the Holy Spirit indwells us. It is possible for any Christian to even end up in prison for serious offences should that Christian go their own way (except if there is a law prohibiting the free practice of our faith in various ways and then that law would be applied to those walking in His Spirit as well).

Second, Paul himself is continually correcting the recipients of his missives of their ways; Galatians being an obvious one in the context of this book. The Corinthians also received a verbal barrage for their behaviours and yet these people had experienced the salvation of Christ. On many occasions, Paul's message was simple: stop doing these things, and return to those things I had previously taught you to believe and to do! Yes, there is hope for those willing to again be led by the Holy Spirit.

THE TOO-HARD BASKET

If indeed the Holy Spirit is leading us to our calling of liberty and love, fulfilling the law, then the rest of Galatians 5 takes on an enormous significance in our lives. Some of the verses in the section of the chapter have been quoted on numerous occasions; whereas others have been avoided. How strange!

It is during this passage that Paul emphasises the ultimate punchlines for our daily walk with God. In a previous section above, the significance of the two corollaries in Galatians 5 were foregrounded. In finally arriving at this essay's destination, the focus will now rest upon Galatians 5:18.

Truthfully I can testify that in the five or so decades I have confessed Christ and been part of His *ecclesia* or church, this verse is probably the least spoken about. Once, I even heard a preacher skip over this verse whilst preaching on the rest of Galatians 5, and I was astonished! So as not to disrespect the preacher, I put to you that this particular verse on most occasions would likely end up in the **TOO-HARD BASKET** !

Why? The hardest thing to do as a Christian, whether young or old, is to learn how to be led by the Holy Spirit! (Some might claim it's the easiest.) **Likewise, the hardest thing to do as a Christian apostle, prophet, pastor, teacher or evangelist is to TEACH God's people how to walk in His Spirit.**

This is the main reason why most of the church universal has not done the best job of it on and off for nearly two thousand years – it's just in the too-hard basket! It's especially hard if you yourself are having problems with a legalistic mindset or licentious disposition, or a mixture of both. Often it's our own local or denominational doctrines that prevent us escaping those mindsets or dispositions.

Admittedly, even mentioning being led by His Spirit is for many of us a very scary proposition! For church leaders, it can be scary because as one late pastor of mine once said: *"Anything can happen and it probably will!"* We want all things to be done decently and in order don't we, just as Paul himself told us in 1 Corinthians 14:40?

We not only need self-control, but we feel that we need our churches "under control".

Furthermore, for the lay Christian, the whole idea of 'abandoning' ourselves to the leading of the Creator of the Universe is a little daunting to say the least! Wouldn't it be easier to just be under someone else's control by obeying the people above us in spiritual stature; just doing anything and everything they tell us to do? There is merit in that if you've either placed yourself under law or are struggling with learning to be led by His Spirit. Undoubtedly scripture instructs us to: *"Obey those who rule over you, and be submissive, for they watch out for your souls, as those who must give account. Let them do so with joy and not with grief, for that would be unprofitable for you."* Hebrews chapter 13 verse 17 (NKJV) As a man under authority I cannot help but adhere to this in the assumption that the person ruling over me is being guided by Galatians 5:18 and is teaching me how to walk in His Spirit. My leader isn't always going to be physically with me as I progress along the pilgrim's way. Somewhere along the line I'm going to reach a level of maturity in this according to Romans 8:14; whilst still having a heart posture to be under authority.

Or wouldn't it be easier to just go along my merry way doing what I think is best, and just let God pull me up before I get into trouble with that proverbial neon sign in the sky? In other words, wouldn't it be easier for us to resort to either legalism or licence or both and just look like we're being Christians most of the time?

I hope that we can see the flaws in some of these statements having studied the concepts above.

The one thing that we need to have in our own walk with God is authenticity; we want to prevent being influenced by the doctrines of what I call 'pseudo-Christianity'.

Pseudo-Christianity looks like Christianity, sounds like Christianity and even smells like Christianity but is its aim here on Earth, whilst we still have human breath, to actually teach us how to be led by the Holy Spirit; thereby leading us to maturity?

Amongst many others, what could be one indicator of this maturity in Christ that we seek? As I noted in a devotional back in 2006, the mark of maturity in Christians is partly measured by the way in which they respond to the sins and mistakes they themselves commit; and then the sins and mistakes others commit. I have been chewing over Galatians chapter six and verse one for many years now!

[ON A PERSONAL NOTE

Please don't think for one moment that the author of this thesis has not struggled and does not struggle with all of this. When I was visiting Russia over twenty years ago, I learned that the word 'confession' is equivalent to the western concept of a 'denomination', as one confesses their faith in league with other like-minded and like-hearted brothers and sisters in Christ. My confession is a little more personal, putting me at risk of being my own 'denomination'. I confess that I have, like Paul in Romans 7, battled with the Holy Spirit with my own flesh; scoring a pyrrhic victory on most occasions. In other words I ultimately lost out in those battles, but it gave me the desire to allow the Holy Spirit to win the next battle for my own and everyone else's benefit! I wanted to get back to being led by His Spirit ASAP.

One recent quote from Ps John Bevere has helped me considerably with this battle: "We have not brought a healthy balance of the holy fear of God into the church. The love of God keeps us from legalism and we don't want legalism 'cause that kills. But the fear of God keeps us from falling into the trap of lawlessness." (Facebook: Adam Hagaman, retrieved 10/6/25)

Rest complete – release the vehicle!]

THE SAMPLE BASKET

So, what could being led by the Spirit look like should we take it out of the too-hard basket? The one idea that we need to be gripped by is that being led by His Spirit, for Christians, is more natural and earthy than we think. It's often said that we Christians are 'supernaturally natural'. Let's not forget that the Lord of the Universe arrived on the scene as a *bona fide* flesh, bone and blood *homo sapiens sapiens* (excuse all the Latin). You could not get both more spiritual and more earthy than the Son of Man!

That said, let's take a modern example of how we walk in His Spirit or be led by His Spirit. All through this book you have been 'driving your car' and most of us would consider that we are fairly competent drivers; albeit I can guarantee that very few of us have actually asked God to make us better ones!

The clause 'walking in the Spirit' seems to be a generic term denoting any action we might undertake as a human being. So for the purpose of our divine drive, we shall now adjust the clause to 'driving in the spirit', without adding to or subtracting from scripture (Cf. Revelation 22: 18, 19). (One could adapt the clause to become 'worshipping in the Spirit', 'praying in the Spirit', 'singing in the Spirit', 'playing sport in the Spirit', 'loving my wife in the Spirit' – surely being led by the Spirit would cover most if not every activity in a Christian's life?).

Now most Christians might assume that 'driving in the Spirit' would include the following:

- switching on your favourite worship song;
- raising one hand in the air as you sing along (you don't quite trust Jesus yet to be fully steering the vehicle);
- and you have one eye closed so that everyone will know that you're spiritual, the other eye keeping you from both scoring a traffic fine and bumping into your pastor's motorbike in the church carpark;
- You may also have something Christian dangling from the front mirror to assure yourself that reaching your destination was really quite miraculous after all!

Sorry, readers, I beg to differ. The above description, albeit all very helpful things to do under most other circumstances does not necessarily denote 'driving in the Spirit'.

For me 'driving in the Spirit' is much less complicated than all of this:

- before I open the door, I scan around to make sure the area is clear of other vehicles or persons (I'm sounding like a police officer now);
- I repeat this process once I'm in the driver's seat and after I have secured myself with the seat belt (I can then put my favourite worship song on, but this is not compulsory by law);
- I start the engine, then proceed to do the things that will get me safely to my destination – stopping at stop signs; giving way to others as permitted; keeping to the speed limits and not showing off 30 kph above the limit to impress my friends or even myself; not manually using my mobile phone (it's not supposed to be mobile

in a car); following instructions from authority figures as required; then arriving at my destination safely.

HANG ON! Just wait a minute! (Here come the keyboard warriors.) Haven't you done what every other driver, Christian or otherwise, is required to do? And you have the nerve to tell us that this is the essence of 'driving in the Spirit'? Surely closing one eye in traffic isn't that bad! Hmmmmmmmm.

Indeed the answer is found not far after reading Galatians 5:18. In fact we come across one of the most read passages in God's Word: chapter 5 and verses 19 to 23. The first three of these verses refers to the 'works of the flesh' (NKJV) and surely you can pick two or three of those characteristics at least to describe how some people drive!

THE FRUIT OF THE SPIRIT

One of the most amazing aspects of the fruit of the Spirit is that *"Against such there is no law."* (Gal. 5:23 NKJV) Isn't it wonderful to know that we are free to grow this fruit as much as we would like without usually having to face a magistrate! Let's examine two aspects of this fruit, against which there are no constraints.

It's interesting to note that the list presented to us in chapter 5 verses 22 and 23 is book-ended by **LOVE** and **SELF-CONTROL** (well that one ends in an **L** at least). Let's take a brief look at the latter first. With most road statistics, we find that there has been a certain proportion of road deaths attributed to drunkenness, speed and other distracting behaviours. If the causes of these tragedies were categorised, you could come to the conclusion that many of these deaths or injuries could have been prevented with a dose of good old-fashioned **SELF-CONTROL** (and maybe a lot of patience or longsuffering here as well; another element of the fruit of His Spirit). Self-control is a vital part of the fruit of the Spirit, as it helps to negate any excessive behaviour that we might be predisposed to overexaggerate in other parts of the fruit.

So where does **LOVE** play a part in 'driving in the Spirit'?

First, I am a blessed man who has loved ones. Jill, my wife, would like me to survive the journey so she can continue loving on me and me on her. She doesn't want that frightening knock on the door from the local constabulary. She wants me home with her. This is love and informs my motivation for driving competently and safely.

Second, if I have my loved ones with me in the car, I want to drive with love and self-control to get them home safely.

Third, the drivers and passengers in other vehicles also have loved ones, either in the car or at home waiting for them. It is not only imperative for them to drive demonstrating the fruit of the Spirit for their own sake, but it is vital that they at least drive with self-control for my and my family's sake as well and vice versa.

A CREATION PRINCIPLE OR LAW?

How then do we fulfil the law, as in Galatians 5:14? We serve one another in love, and this applies on the road for absolutely anyone, regardless of spiritual commitment. Does this lessen the importance of being led by the Spirit for Christians? No. But it does serve to remind us that over 8 billion people on this planet presently are living in a world created by God; a world that operates on God's **CREATION PRINCIPLES**, whether we want them to or not! After all *"...He makes His sun rise on the evil and on the good, and sends rain on the just and on the unjust."* (Matthew 5:45).

It is well to remember that allowing God to grow the fruit of His Spirit in our lives applies to ALL things.

LEGALISM, LAWLESSNESS OR LOVE ON OUR ROADS?

If I am a born again, Spirit-filled new creation, why do I still obey certain laws, like road laws, and not obey others?

What then distinguishes the heart of those who want to be led by the Holy Spirit when driving a car from those who are not even thinking that way? When we come across a sign indicating that a section of road should only be driven at a maximum speed of 60 kph (that's 35 mph for our American and UK friends) what is usually the first thing that comes into our minds, especially if we know there's a police car lurking in the bushes somewhere and I've been doing 65?

"Oh no, I'm going to be pulled over by the cops! I'm going to get fined. I haven't got my licence on me. I'm going to lose all my points. I can't do my job if I haven't got my licence! The wife's going to kill me (so much for loving on me)!"

If you're doing well over 60, or even just a little over 60 in one particular state of Australia that shall go unnamed, the panic can hit you like a runaway truck. You can feel the bile rising up from your gut and you know you've been very naughty indeed.

Essentially this is legalism on the roads. It is based solely on the transaction of breaking the law and being punished for it. It is usually accompanied by feelings of guilt and shame. Many of us have experienced this little transaction that ends up with your jurisdiction getting richer and you getting poorer. The problem is that most people are motivated by this form of legalism to be 'under the law' to save themselves from being punished. This brings back memories of the lowest level of Kohlberg's hierarchy of moral development (Cherry, 2025) [33], albeit superseded by other developmental models. Legalism causes people to want to avoid punishment in the context of road usage. This is obviously not 'driving in the Spirit'.

In the last few years in our state of Queensland in north eastern Australia, we have had a bout of tragedies on our roads all with similar characteristics. In one such incident (Siganto, 2022) [34] a drug-affected youth stole a vehicle and recklessly drove it through red lights, damaging other cars and ultimately driving it into a couple at traffic lights on a corner waiting to cross the road. The young woman was pregnant. All three, the father, mother and her unborn child, were killed in this incident. The man's grieving father was recently elected into the state parliament (congress) endeavouring to give a voice to the victims of similar tragedies and to secure appropriate penalties for the perpetrators.

This is a situation that perfectly describes licence or lawlessness. Apparently the perpetrator gave himself permission to firstly take illegal substances and get 'off his face' as the saying goes; to steal a vehicle, drive it in an insane manner and then kill three people, albeit unwittingly. This whole incident could be described biblically as 'works of the flesh'. There was definitely no 'driving in the Spirit' here or any motivation to love anyone. For erratic drivers, there are two types of licence: the one the state gives them and the one they give themselves; albeit in this case ironically, the driver was also unlicenced – above the law.

LEGALISM, LAWLESSNESS OR LOVE ON OUR ROADS?

Although I would not consider myself to be the most skilful driver in the world (just ask one of my sons-in-law), I nevertheless desire to 'drive in the Spirit'; to drive in such a manner whereby godly love for myself and other people is my main motivation. Kohlberg would call that maturity, the top level of moral development being referred to as Principle. This is the difference between the mindset involved in being led by the Spirit and the mindset utilised in legalism or lawlessness.

I have no desire to drive legalistically and be under constant fear of punishment and I certainly have no desire to do my own thing on the roads; placing myself and other people in harm's way regardless of how skilful I think I am as a driver. A 100 kph speed limit is there for a reason; to keep people as safe as possible. It is not there to annoy the people who have a sense of entitlement.

THE PRIMARY CONCEPT

Most Christians have a 'favourite' verse or passage of scripture for a variety of reasons, regardless of the teaching that all scripture is equally valuable. It's only natural that there are certain verses that impact us more deeply than others; they are very personal from a personal God.

My favourite, if you haven't already worked it out, is Galatians 5:18, complementary to my personal mission statement. I regard this one as enshrining the primary concept for our existence on Earth before we meet our Maker in the aeon to come.

> **The concept of 'walking in His Spirit' or 'being led by His Spirit' encompasses ALL our thoughts, motivations, utterances and actions as a Christian.**

> **BEING LED BY THE SPIRIT ENABLES US TO:**
> Experience Love, Joy and Peace;
> Enact Patience, Kindness and Goodness;
> Empower Faithfulness, Meekness and Self-Control;
> (Remembering that it is God who is growing this fruit in the good soil of our hearts; not us!);
> Be awed in and by God's Holiness;

Worship and Sing in His Spirit;
Pray and Intercede in His Spirit;
Pray for and follow our spiritual leaders as they endeavour
to set an example to us of being led by His Spirit;
"Rightly divide the Word of Truth";
Fellowship with our Contemporary Saints;
Meet the needs of these Saints, both spiritually and naturally;
Give in and outside of the church
(applying Gal. 5:18 to this one leads to an interesting conversation!);
Share His Gospel; and
Go about our everyday tasks with purpose.
(Please feel free to add to this list.)

Without being led by His Spirit we are not able to experience any of these amazing facets of Christ's life in us. After all, *"...it is no longer I who live, but Christ lives in me..."* (Gal. 2:20 NKJV)

'BREATHING IN THE SPIRIT'

In order to live there are certain functions that we need to keep our earthly bodies going: breathing, eating, drinking; along with other natural functions. Having given myself permission to talk about 'driving in the Spirit', it could be just as appropriate for me to discuss 'breathing in the Spirit', 'eating in the Spirit' and 'drinking in the Spirit'. The Bible talks constantly about all the functions mentioned above; both naturally and spiritually.

So how does Christ live in us, as in Galatians 2:20? Realistically there are functions being performed by Christ in us to help us keep going in His Spirit, namely:

He is constantly breathing into us and over us; *"And when He had said this, he breathed on them, and said to them, 'Receive the Holy Spirit.' "* (John 20: 22 NKJV). The word 'spirit' is derived from Latin and actually means 'breath'. The very first act of man was to take a breath from the nostrils of God Himself.

He is constantly feeding us; when speaking to Peter to test his heart posture, *"He said to him the third time, 'Son of Jonah, do you love Me?' And he said to Him, 'Lord, You know all things; You know that I love You.' Jesus said to him, 'Feed My sheep.' "* (John 21:17 NKJV)

He is constantly enabling us to drink; when speaking to the Samaritan woman at Jacob's well, *"Jesus answered and said to her, 'Whoever drinks of this water will thirst again, but whoever drinks of the water that I shall give him will never thirst. But the water that I shall give him will become in him a fountain of water springing up into everlasting life.'* " (John 4: 13, 14 NKJV)

As we breath, eat and drink in Christ, we shall experience the crucified and resurrected faith life in Christ emphasised in Galatians 2: 19, 20 (NKJV).

THE EVERYDAY TASKS

In his book *You Can Do It!* (Wade, 1976) [35] - a transcript of a series taught in our local church in Wagga Wagga NSW at the time-, the late Rev. Peter Wade challenged yours truly to touch my ear with my elbow (ibid., p9). I remember feeling disappointed that I couldn't meet the challenge (another ego-deflating moment for this young man). He shared my disappointment but reassured me that there will always be some things we'll never be able to do (unless you're a contortionist). This, despite reading Philippians chapter 4 verse 13: *"I can do all things through Christ who strengthens me."* (NKJV)

The Concordant Literal NT renders this as: *"For (sic)* ***all am I strong in Him Who is (sic) invigorating me – Christ!"*** As Christians we can be full of "vim, vigour and vitality" as we used to say.

Upon digesting this verse, many of us might think that this only refers to spiritual things: giving a person a divinely-led word of encouragement; praying for your friend's healing; receiving a specific word from the Bible regarding your circumstances. All of these are common for Christians and this constitutes much of what we see as the main things in which God can provide strength or 'unction' as used by many believers in the past. We definitely need the leading of the Spirit to do ALL of these things. There is no argument here.

Yet if we read verse 13 in context, which is always a great exegetical thing to do, we shall discover that Paul was also referring to some natural everyday occurrences as well. When talking about the provision made for him by the saints in Philippi, he explains: *"I know how to be abased, and I know how to abound. EVERYWHERE and in ALL THINGS* (capitals mine) *I have learned both to be full and to be hungry, both to abound and to suffer need."* (NKJV). It is vital to note that St Paul was able to do all things in Christ's strength, regardless of his circumstances.

At the risk of stretching a point too far, I wonder just what sorts of needs you are 'suffering' right now. This can get very practical indeed, and may not seem very different to what your atheist or agnostic neighbours' needs are. A human need is a human need after all! Just ask the victim in Jesus' parable of *The Good Samaritan* (Luke 10: 25 – 37).

It was a custom in our group of Christian schools to lead students in prayer before they sat down to do an exam (as well as many other things). We often forget to ask God for strength in the everyday things that we need to do. (By the way, in the context of an exam, this is not cheating! We're merely asking God for the strength to action the task before us and to provide the level of mental and physical health needed to accomplish what we've set out to do. God is not an illegal, performance-enhancing drug!)

Being led by the Spirit or walking in the Spirit cannot be timetabled into our day like we used to do in Christian schooling. It is not a separate subject in our lives that is devoid of all the other things in our lives. Yes, we can be taught to 'wait upon the Lord' for a divinely-inspired word for someone, but we also need to be taught how to be led by the Spirit when we are working out a quadratic equation; or we are struggling to obey the teacher because our home lives are not ideal; or when we are made to stand up in assembly to our great embarrassment and clap along to a boring old song (this applies to the students as well!); or we are tempted during a

History lesson to go into the bathrooms with all the cool dudes and vape our brains into oblivion (applying only to certain students)! THAT'S when we need to resort to being led by the Spirit as much as any seemingly spiritual activity; this being at the very junction of this little thesis.

So when you have a need of any sort, remind yourself that:
"I can do all things through Christ who strengthens me!"

HOLY SPIRIT AWARENESS

Most experienced Christians would admit that on many occasions they are not aware that they are being led by His Holy Spirit. Obviously we choose to be led but we're not always conscious of the process involved, of how it is taking place and even if it's taking place at all (cf. John 3:8 in the context of not knowing where the Spirit is blowing).

I am reminded of old biblical movies I used to watch; you know the monochrome ones with the grainy reception and actors who are now non-living legends – take a bow Charlton Heston and fellow thespians! In hindsight I am amused at how 'spiritual' they all seemed; those faraway looks searching for God beyond the clouds and the way they walked as if they had starch in their underpants. Yes, they were indeed endeavouring to capture the grandeur and awe of God; yet I doubt I could pull those behaviours off these days without attracting unwanted attention!

Obviously this is not the way we see 'walking in the Spirit' nowadays. You never know, it could be happening in your life right now and you'd never know it. Sometimes you will know and be able to follow the steps God placed before you; sometimes we shall never know until this dispensation is wrapped up.

I once went through a discipleship year of study with a young man in his early twenties who was baptised in the Holy Spirit one evening whilst reading a *DC* comic! Yes, you read that correctly. Now that's not something we would normally encourage people to do at an altar call, as many dissenters might point out, and it even surprised and amused the most 'spiritual' Christians in our church at that time. He had gone to the front for prayer at our annual convention and had 'received' nothing of note from the Lord at that time. But afterwards when he was relaxed in the comfort of his own home and with his own thoughts, God met him in a special way in His good time. This young man was filled with the Spirit with the ability to speak in a divine language; a private offering to God. Although his comic book may not have been part of God's plan, it happened in the context of a 'normal' setting.

So then *we walk by faith and not by sight* as Paul's second letter to the Corinthians points out in chapter 5 and verse 7. Awareness will not always accompany us in our walk.

THE 'TREE OF THE KNOWLEDGE OF WALKING IN THE SPIRIT'?

It's a sure thing that this true little story will attract a tsunami of critics. It's a story that has not gained global recognition and is unlikely to do so unless we make the *New York Times* Bestseller List.

Nevertheless, there is a significant point to make here. Even in the realm of those endeavouring to be led by His Spirit or walking in the Spirit, there are those who will approach all of this as religious legalists or as those given an opportunity to use it for their flesh life; as the Galatians received warning in chapter 5 verse 13.

This is perhaps the most dangerous aspect of our walk with Jesus: that we so easily drift from the realm of the divine into our own little pseudo-Christian world; that we begin to make up our own rules/laws/whatever to contain the sovereignty of God in a usable and convenient format. We may even be able to package this and market it to the world. I'm probably in danger of doing that myself with this book; an aspect of my life that I have prayed and agonised over for quite a while. Lord, please protect me from my own ego and let Your Truth shine through!

In the meantime we need to look out for the starchy underpants vigilantes; and with a Juan Carlos Ortiz Hispanic accent, wrap them in our love with a *"we don't argue, we just hug you!"*

LAW OR EXPEDIENCE?

Right in the middle of rebukes for sexual immorality and other activities, Paul points out in his first letter to the Corinthian assembly, chapter 6 and verse 12 that *All things are lawful for me, but all things are not helpful. All things are lawful for me, but I will not be brought under the power of any.* (NKJV) In chapter 10 and verse 23, he repeats the same concept in a slightly different context.

The Con Lit NT puts 6:12 this way: *All is allowed me, but not all is expedient. All is allowed me, but I will not be put under its authority by anything.*

In walking in His Holy Spirit, who or what is sovereign over our desires? Is it law or lawlessness, or is it that which is most helpful for me? Obviously from the context of these verses, all is lawful or permitted; maybe even morally accessible to me (do we have a DANGER sign on this journey?); albeit, as discussed in the section concerning **COMMANDS**, I am under authority, just like the Roman centurion whose faith impressed Jesus. Although I am not under law, I am still subject to God's CREATION PRINCIPLES, for: *Be not deceived, God is not to be sneered at, for whatsoever a man may be sowing, this shall he be reaping also, for he who is sowing for his own flesh, from the flesh shall be reaping corruption, yet he who is sowing for the spirit, from the spirit shall be reaping life eonian.* Galatians 6:7,8 (Con Lit NT)

This is the proper basis of what is known as 'moral law'; without being under law. Believe it or not, it has taken even this Christian a long time to work this one through in his own life.

There is a beautiful example of this type of expediency in Mike Pence's book *So Help Me God* (Pence, 2022) [36]. The former Vice President of the United States took inspiration from the late Rev Billy Graham (ibid., pp 62-63) by expediently choosing not to dine with any lady alone other than his own wife (ibid. pp 218-220). It sure saved Vice President Pence a heap of heartache, especially with the Press, but the key thing to note here is that there was no law preventing him from doing otherwise; his own heart of love fulfilled the law by allowing the Holy Spirit's wisdom to guide him.

Such is the wisdom that God provides when we choose to be led by His Spirit.

Being a **Wise Galatian** is not always about miraculous power; it's just as much about having your character developed.

THE UNVEILED FACE

In discussing all of the matters above we have cut a wide swathe of issues. Then again, if walking in the Spirit or being led by the same does not cover everything, then I have just spent the last forty or so years spiritually and intellectually dribbling into my bib.

So what was starting to happen to our brothers and sisters in Galatia almost two millennia ago? They were starting to lose sight of the reality to which Paul had introduced them and gaps were being formed in their Christian worldview. They were forgetting what they looked like in the mirror: *"the perfect law of liberty"*. (James 1: 23 – 25 NKJV)

The letter to the Galatians was written to remind them of what they really looked like in Christ. The veil is taken away, as St Paul reminds us in 2 Corinthians 3 and verses 16 to 18 (NKJV): ***"Nevertheless when one turns to the Lord, the veil is taken away. Now the Lord is the Spirit; and where the Spirit of the Lord is, there is liberty. But we all with unveiled face, beholding as in a mirror the glory of the Lord, are being transformed into the same image from glory to glory, just as by the Spirit of the Lord.***

THE WISE GALATIANS

If being a foolish Galatian will never enable me to be what I was always meant to be, and will always position me to receive a thorough dressing down from the likes of the apostle Paul, then maybe it would be in my best interest to become a **wise Galatian** instead!

What then is **THE** number one topic that needs to be taught, especially to those new to faith in Christ? If it were so easy for the early church with relatively novice pastors and teachers to 'mission drift' in the area of the leading of the Holy Spirit, maybe we should consider that being led by the Holy Spirit will prevent that drift. Should this not then be the major topic of our instruction to young and old, seeing that 'walking in the Spirit' is our umbrella activity for all that we think, say and do to keep us out from 'under law', and that 'being led by the Holy Spirit' is the very activity that will bring about our maturity according to Romans chapter 8 verse 14? *"After all, teaching new Christians how to live for Christ is as much a part of Christ's commission as winning them – Matthew 28: 19-20)."* (Wiersbe, 1975) [37]

Let's again consider the imagery of Frudakis' sculpture in Philadelphia. Although the chosen image does not show the extreme right-hand figure, you can rest assured that it has totally broken free from the stone slab that kept it imprisoned. Do we really want liberty? Do we really want love? **What do we really desire?** Remember Uncle Ben's rebuke to Toby Mcguire's budding *Spiderman* [38]: *"With great power comes great responsibility."* ? We could equally substitute 'power' with 'liberty' or 'love'. We do have a responsibility to learn how to be led by Christ's Spirit, and to teach it, even though it could be viewed as a great burden.

It was never the intention of this book to reveal the unlimited ways in which that can be done; merely to lay a doctrinal foundation for the church universal. I shall leave the more detailed teaching to those who have gone before me and to my contemporaries and to those who may follow on. Avail yourself of relevant books and have those meaningful conversations with your leaders. Like Paul, someone may have to *labour in birth again until Christ is formed in you.* (NKJV) The Con Lit NT uses the word *travailing*.

To what specifically was the apostle Paul connecting this 'reforming' of Christ in the Galatian believers? It was the way in which they were endeavouring to be made perfect (NKJV) or complete (Con Lit NT). Aren't we all interested in this? The Galatians were trying to be made perfect or complete through their flesh life having already received the Spirit by the hearing of faith (Gal. 3:2). Paul is simply exhorting them strongly to continue their walk in the Spirit by that same hearing of faith.

YOU BEGAN THIS WAY ~ CONTINUE THIS WAY!

It behoves us all to continue in this Way.

I shall leave you with a scripture that gels beautifully with this thought and relieves us of the burden we may feel with the responsibility this bestows on us:

> *"Come to Me, all you (sic) who labor and are heavy laden, and I will give you rest. Take my yoke upon you and learn*

from Me, for I am gentle and lowly in heart, and (sic) *you will find rest for your souls. For My yoke is easy and My burden is light."* (Matthew chapter 11: 28-30 NKJV)

Nothing could be better than to learn to be led by His Spirit by actually being yoked to Jesus! Allow yourself now to be yoked to Him so that you can **be completed in the Holy Spirit.**

"Catch you soon, everyone – my name is Geoff - and I am now a **WISE GALATIAN !**" (*Some applauding.*) "We're with you, Geoff! Hallelujah! Praise the Lord, brother!"

Thank you for taking this journey with me. Now please pull over safely into your final parking bay - without getting into a fight with the bloke who was about to steal your spot; especially after everything we've talked about!

REFERENCES

PART ONE - BACKGROUND

1. Greer, P and Horst, C. (2014) *Mission Drift* South Bloomington MN Bethany House Publishers.
2. Harrison, S. A. (Gen. Ed. et al) (2015) *NLT Illustrated Study Bible* Wheaton Ill. Tyndale House Publishers Inc.
3. Begg, A. (2021) *The Man on the Middle Cross Said I Can Come.* Available at: https://www.bing.com/videos/riverview.relatedvideo?q=alistair%20begg%20man%20on %20the%20 cross&mid=054DAC1867227DE62F85054DAC-1867227DE62F85&ajaxhist=0

PART TWO - SHAKY GROUND

4. Smith, T. (2008) *A Pharisee of Pharisees.* Available at: https://www.catholicnewsagency.com/author/35/thomas-smith (Accessed: 18 January 2025).
5. Smith, T. (13 October 2008) *Roman Citizen in a Greek-influenced Culture.* Available at:

https://www.catholicnewsagency.com/author/35/thomas-smith (Accessed: 18 January 2025).
6. Available at: https://www.azquotes.com/author/14541-Tertullian?p=3 (Accessed: 18 January 2025).
7. Moore, B. ed. (2001) *The Australian Pocket Oxford Dictionary.* 5 th edn. South Melbourne, Vic.: Oxford University Press.
8. Australian Constitution Centre *Principle 2: The Rule of Law.* Available at: https://www.australianconstitutioncentre.org.au (Accessed: 6 June 2024).
9. Blight, Ps G. (16 January 2023) Life Church, Salisbury, Qld. Used with permission.
10. Tait, C. (2023) *What is the Law in the Bible and its Purpose?* FIRM (Fellowship of Israel Related Ministries) Available at: *firmisrael.org* (Accessed: 17 January 2025).
11. Copland, D. (2025) *Killing the CEO,* Mona Vale NSW: Ark House Press.
12. Mayo Clinic (2023) *Obsessive Compulsive Disorder.* Available at: https://www.mayoclinic.org/diseases-conditions/obsessive-compulsive-disorder/symptons-causes/syc-20354432#:~:text=?Obsessive-compulsive (Accessed: 18 January 2025).
13. Gay, G. (2019) *LostRalia.* Mona Vale NSW: Ark House Press.
14. Ryken, P. (2023) *How Many Israelites Exited Egypt?* Available at: https://www.thegospelcoalition.org/article/how-many-israelites-exited-egypt/ (Accessed: 16 January 2025).
15. Solberg, Prof. R.L. (2025) *Is the Law of Moses Eternal?* Available at: https://rlsolberg.com (Accessed: 16 January 2025)
16. Young, Dr R. (1939) *Analytical Concordance to the Holy Bible.* 8 th edn. London UK: Lutterworth Press.

REFERENCES

17. AG Staff. (2024) *Defining Moments in Australian History: Last man hanged.* Available at: https://www.australiangeographic.com.au/topics/science-environment/2024/11/takayna-tarkine (Accessed 17 February 2025)
18. Pritchard, Dr S. (2017) *Digging Wells or Building Fences.* Available at: https://shalomcarcoar.com/2017/02/12/digging-wells-or-building-fences (Accessed: 6 December 2024).
19. Sproul, R C (2016) *3 Types of Legalism.* Available at: https://www.ligonier.org/blog/3-types-legalism/ (Accessed 11 March 2021).
20. Keller, T. (2008) *The Prodigal God.* London UK: Hodder & Stoughton Ltd.
21. Frudakis, Z. (2001) *Freedom Sculpture. Available at* https://www.architecturaldigest.com/gallery/11-most-fascinating-public-sculptures (Accessed 6 June 2021)
22. Gooding, D. (1962) *New Testament Word Studies – Teknon, Huios.* Available at: https://www.preciousseed.org/articles/new-testament-word-studies-teknon-huios/ PS Digital. (Accessed 14 January 2025)
23. Cook, Ps. B. (6 April 1996) *Morning Sermon* Southside Christian Renewal Centre (now Life Church), Salisbury Queensland Australia.
24. Green, C 'Kitty' (2024) *Licence to Love: Driven by Faith.* Enumclaw WA: Redemption Press.
25. Mumford, Rev. R. (1973) *The Problem of Doing Your Own Thing.* Fort Lauderdale Fl: Christian Growth Ministries.
26. Lloyd D. (1973) *The Idea of Law.* Middlesex UK: Penguin Books Ltd.
27. Golding, W. (1954) *Lord of the Flies.* London UK: Faber & Faber Ltd.

28. applesdontpee (2020) *Galatians Syndrome symbolism.* Available at: Galatians Syndrome symbolism : r/bladerunner www.reddit.com (Accessed: 5 December 2024)
29. Moyo, D. (2025) *Keep it out of reach if its* (sic) *not from God!* Available at: https://www.facebook.com/prophetdelroymoyo/ (Accessed 18 February 2025).
30. Sutter, K. (Creator) (2008 – 2014) *Sons of Anarchy*, Fox 21 et al. USA.
31. Balingit, M. – AP (2025) *Some US lawmakers want more Christianity in the classroom. Trump could embolden their plans.* Available at: (Accessed: 14 January 2025)

PART THREE ~ FOREGROUND

32. *Spartacus Roman Gladiator* (ed. 2025) Available at: *https://www.brittanica.com/biography/Spartacus-Roman-gladiator* (Accessed: 14 February 2025)

PART FOUR ~ TAKING GROUND

33. Cherry, K. (2025) *Kohlberg's Theory of Moral Development - How we learn to tell right from wrong.* Available at: https://www.verywellmind.com/kohlbergs-theory-of-moral-development-2795071 (Accessed 4 December 2024)
34. Siganto, T. (2022). *Teen jailed for killing pregnant Katherine Leadbetter and partner Matthew Field in Alexandra Hills hit-and-run.* Available at: Teen jailed for killing pregnant Katherine Leadbetter and partner Matthew Field in Alexandra Hills hit-and-run - ABC News (Accessed 14 January 2025)
35. Wade, P. (1976) *You Can Do It!* Adelaide SA: The Word, Inc.

REFERENCES

36. Pence, Mike (2022) *So Help Me God*. New York NY: Simon & Schuster Paperbacks.
37. Wiersbe, WW (1975) *Be Free*. Wheaton, Ill: Victor Books.
38. Koepp, David (2002) *Spiderman*, Columbia Pictures et al., USA.

AFTERWORD

After finally finishing this little book, my main piece of advice is: think twice before you do the same! If your chief source of inspiration is the Bible itself, you're automatically going to have a problem, that being: what do I leave out? This book is centred around the Letter to the Galatians, but, like any effective sporting team, for example, you need all the other players alongside you for any meaningful plays. With the Bible I could have brought so many other 'players' (verses from other books) off the bench and onto the field of play, but I felt led to only use those ones that helped to explain specific concepts. For this I apologise to genuine theologians who may have been expecting a PhD-like tome on the subject. This book is just a drop in the bucket of many books that have and might yet be written on this and similar themes (cf. John 21:25).

For those who may like to attempt such a task, and especially those who may have taken umbrage at my personal understanding of the themes of God's Word, please imitate the Berean Jews who went home and did their own research. If any concept needs clarifying, by all means contact me if you can find me. I think I look forward to hearing from you!

Please note that this book was not negatively aimed at any particular local church, denomination, church or para-church movement or any person or persons. As mentioned above, this book was written to encourage the church universal: all my contemporary believers!

Also, as mentioned, the sweep of church history has not been covered, as that will only give us an idea of the issues pertaining to those days. There have been two thousand years worth of 'issues of the day'. To delve into all or some of those issues would undermine the key message of this book – that of being led by the Holy Spirit in the context of 'any issues of the day'. Likewise I have rarely mentioned the many brothers and sisters who have unwittingly contributed in various ways to the theme of this book; including the likes of Martin Luther. I believe God has other things for me to do in the limited time I have left on this planet, so I'll let you write those volumes instead of me to obtain your PhD's. Suffice to say that no matter at what time in the grace dispensation God introduced His Word to you, you would still have to grapple with what it means to be led by His Spirit in God's general will for your life and/or the particular context of the time and space in which He has placed you. This is what I have attempted to do in this brief study for me and my contemporaries.

Furthermore, this book generates more questions than answers. I do not claim to be the fount of wisdom for all situations and circumstances; hence I shall not be giving you advice concerning the business loan you believe God wants you to take on; or worse, confirming that the cute guy leading worship is going to be your husband! Better folk than I are leading churches and Christian institutions and it would be expedient for you to avail yourself of the wisdom God has granted them.

Finally, I consider this book to be a conversation with you concerning observations I have gathered over the years rather than a scholarly soliloquy. One of its aims is to initiate discussions around a topic that has been put to one side in various ways for nearly two thousand years since one of those first 'mission drifts'.

ACKNOWLEDGMENTS

As the old adage goes: *it takes a village to raise a child*; I'm guessing that a similar type of village also raises a writer. I acknowledge that in putting this work together I am fulfilling two words of encouragement spoken over me many years ago – call them prophecies if you will - but I am keeping those words close to my heart as Jesus's mother Mary did whilst Christ was formed in her just over two millenia ago.

To Lauren Oduko who drew the little roadside illustrations: thank you so much for your time, effort and generosity. May your career as an author and illustrator be as stellar as your talent.

To Emma McLachlan, a brilliant English teacher, thank you for 'driving' through my first draft with love, long suffering and self-control. Your succinct appraisal was most encouraging; as I know it is with all of your students.

To those at Ark House Press (Initiate Media) who partnered with me to give me both my first and second publishing experiences, I am most grateful. Thank you James Newman, Nicole Danswan, John Philips and all their team for accommodating me.

To those I have earbashed in staff rooms, classrooms and lounge rooms over the last forty-odd years, thank you for your forbearance and your eye-rolls. You, the village of Christ, have helped me grow as a person and in understanding His general and/or contextual will.

To my long-suffering wife, Jill; what an amazing woman! Your growth in the fruit of the Holy Spirit has always been my lifeline to prevent me from drifting. To our children and their own families, thank you that I get to be your dad and Grandpa Geoff in a world where homes and families are desperately crying out for liberty and love in the Holy Spirit.

And to Lord God my Father, Jesus my Lord Brother through His shed blood and resurrection, and my Lord Holy Spirit the Comforter, without you I am nothing – with you I am someone! Thank you.

ABOUT THE AUTHOR

Geoffrey Gay is a retired schoolteacher who has invested most of his career into imparting his life-experience in Christian schools and in other contexts around Australia and abroad. His students have ranged in age from five to fifty-five in subjects such as introductory classical Latin, History, Geography, Civics, Legal Studies, Colouring-in and Sandbox! His first book, **LostRalia** *(Ark House Press)*, is an anachronistic allegorical narrative poem presented in the epic tradition; reflecting some of the concepts found in this book. Geoffrey lives with his wife of forty-five years, Jill, and their coffee-coloured toy poodle, Merlo, in a quaint little cottage in Brisbane. They are always boasting about their four married children, their four children-in-law, their ten grandchildren and two granddaughters-in-law.

www.ingramcontent.com/pod-product-compliance
Lightning Source LLC
LaVergne TN
LVHW041624070426
835507LV00008B/444